Índice

Introducción 7
Historia del masaje relajante 9
Medicina ayurveda 13
Definición del masaje terapéutico 15
   A quién va dirigido el masaje relajante 16
Contraindicaciones 19
Atmósfera, equipos y accesorios 21
Preparación antes del masaje 27
Decúbito 31
Drapear 34
Técnicas básicas del masaje terapéutico 37
Higiene postural del masajista o terapeuta 47
   Cuidado de las manos 49
Moral, ética y valores 51

Secuencia del masaje (50 minutos) 57
   Comienzo del masaje 58
   Posición prono (bocabajo) 59
      Espalda 59
      Hombros 69
      Cráneo o Cabeza 73
      Brazos 76
      Piernas - visión posterior 80
   Posición decúbito supino (bocarriba) 92
      Cabeza y cara 92
      Masajes en la cabeza 94
      Masajes en la cara 96
      Hombros, cuello y pectorales 101
      Brazo posterior 106
      Pierna - visión anterior 112

Masaje opcional 123
   Abdomen y pies 123
      Abdomen 123
      Pies 128

Cierre de la sesión de masaje 132

Despedida del cliente 137

Terapias populares de la medicina alternativa. 139
   Terapias alternativas 140

Patologías y condiciones comunes 151

NETWORKING

for

INTROVERTS

Connections Made Simple

STEFEN REY

Networking for Introverts - Connections Made Simple
Copyright 2025
Stephen R. Burchard

Publisher: LimitLESS Academy
35606 Corte Serena, Cathedral City CA 92234
limitlessacademy.net
stefen@bowtiecoach.com

Editing by: Wendy Fink Robinson

ISBN: 979-8-9931257-3-2 Hardback
ISBN: 979-8-9931257-2-5 Paperback
ISBN: 979-8-9931257-0-1 eBook
ISBN: 979-8-9931257-1-8 Audiobook

Library of Congress Cataloging in Publication Data
Application pending

All Rights Reserved
All rights to this book, Networking for Introverts - Connections Made Simple are reserved. No part of this text may be reproduced or transmitted in any form; by any means; including electronic or mechanical photocopying, recording, or storing in an electronic retrieval system; uploaded or ingested into any AI Large Language Model (LLM), or otherwise used without prior written permission of this publisher.

Printed in the U.S.A.

Table of Contents

Forward 9
Acknowledgements 11
Introduction 13
Section I - The Work 17
   Chapter 1: Becoming the Networking Ninja 21
      The Unexpected Path: From IT to Reluctant Entrepreneur 22
      The Birth of the Bowtie Coach: How Bowties Became My Brand Identity 27
      From Shy to Strategic: Leveraging Introversion 31
      Building Quiet Confidence: Lessons In Networking and Development 35
   Chapter 2: The Strengths of Introversion 41
      Introvert Superpowers 42
      Harnessing Energy 45
      Redefining Networking 50
   Chapter 3: Foundations of a Networking Mindset 57
      The Power of Stillness and Focus 57
      1. Stillness 58
      2. Inputs 59

3. Distractions 60
4. Exercise 61
RADICAL Focus 63
    1. Remember Your Why 64
    2. Add Time Blocks 64
    3. Delete Notifications 65
    4. Insulate Your Environment 66
    5. Choose One Thing 66
    6. Accountability 67
    7. Limit Your Availability 68
Building a Growth Mindset 69
Chapter 4: Strategic Networking 75
    SAFER Networking 77
    1. Select 78
    2. Allow 79
    3. Find 80
    4. Engage 80
    5. Reflect & Reward 81
Chapter 5 - Building and Sustaining Relationships 85
    Turning Small Talk Into Meaningful Connections 87
    The First Step Is Organization 88
    A Heartfelt Touch 89
    Tools and Strategies to Deepen Relationships 90

The Power of "Face-to-Face" 92
Handwritten Notes 93
Celebrating Your Connections 94
Express Gratitude Publicly and Privately 95

Chapter 6: The Art of Storytelling 99
Part I: Identifying Your Core Stories 101
Part II: Crafting Magnetic Introductions 105
Part III: Storytelling in Sales and
Everyday Networking 106

Chapter 7 - Social Media & Video 109
Understanding the Platforms 111
Crafting a Compelling Video Strategy 113
Building Engagement 115
Measuring Impact 116

Section II - Into Action 119

Chapter 8: Mindset Matters Most 123
The Power of Mindset in Relationship-
Building 125
Stillness and Reflection 126
Inputs and Focus 128
Breaking Patterns and Embracing Growth . 130
Movement, Self-Care & Your
Empowerment Plan 132

Chapter 9: Networking for Introverts 135
Implementing Strategies: Applying the
Networking Framework 137

Evaluation and Adjustment: Reviewing and Improving Tactics 138

Creating Community: Finding and Contributing to Supportive Circles 139

Understanding the Power of Introversion in Networking 140

Building Confidence and Authentic Connections 141

Mastering the Art of Listening and Conversation 143

Leveraging Introverted Networking Strategies 144

Crafting Your Networking Message and Elevator Pitch 145

Building a Networking Strategy 146

Chapter 10: Camera Confidence and Content 149

Dispelling Myths 152

Finding Your Voice 155

Planning Your Content Creation 158

Final Thoughts 160

Conclusion: Becoming Your Best Self 165

The Power of Progress 165

Staying Grounded Amid Success 166

Inviting the Journey 167

Key Points and Takeaways 169

Next Steps 169

Forward

Every now and then, you meet someone whose growth is so intentional and so clearly guided that you can see the hand of God shaping the process. Stefen is one of those people.

I've had the privilege of walking alongside him as his Peak Performance Mindset Coach and welcoming him into Leaders Club, and what has stood out most is not just his determination or his ambition - it's his willingness to be led and to truly apply what he has learned. His journey is marked by humility, resilience, and a deep courage that only grows stronger over time. Watching him step into his calling with clarity and focus has been nothing short of inspiring.

What makes this book powerful is that it reflects that same posture of surrender and stewardship. Stefen writes honestly about the challenges that many introverts face, and he does it without hiding the truth: growth is uncomfortable, stretching is necessary, and becoming who God created you to be requires intention. He doesn't try to be someone else, and he doesn't ask the reader to be someone they're not. Instead, he shows how introversion - when embraced rather than resisted - can become a God-given strength.

This book isn't theory. It's the lived journey of a man who chose to grow, to show up, and to trust that the gifts placed in him were enough. I've seen him put in the work. I've seen him adopt structure, refine his focus, and lean into environments that once felt overwhelming and uncomfortable. And I've also seen the fruit of that obedience: deeper relationships, greater influence, and a more grounded response to extremely challenging situations.

Many of which, by the way, would have been reason enough for him to cancel the completed authorship of this book. But he faced each difficult situation with honesty, grace, and gratitude while he pressed on with his goal of completing what you are now reading today.

Networking for Introverts offers something rare - practical systems wrapped in wisdom, actionable tools supported by genuine character, and a reminder that you don't have to be loud to make an impact. You just need to shepherd what you've been given with intention. Stefen lays out a path to develop more genuine connections by strategically utilizing the way you naturally communicate.

For anyone who has ever felt overlooked, out of place, or unsure how to connect in a noisy world, the pages ahead will give you hope and a plan. They show that influence doesn't require volume. It requires alignment. It requires authenticity. And, as Stefen demonstrates so well, it requires a willingness to show up as the person God designed you to be.

I'm proud of the leader Stefen is and is becoming and I'm grateful to play a part in his success squad. This book is a timely guide for introverts who want to build meaningful connections without compromising who they are.

You're in good hands with what you're about to read.

— **Kamille Rose Taylor**, BCC
Founder, Peak Mind School for Entrepreneurs
Host, The Success & Surrender Podcast

Acknowledgements

This book represents a journey of growth, reflection, and connection, and it would not exist without the support, wisdom, and encouragement of so many people in my life. It is with a heart overflowing with gratitude that I extend my deepest thanks.

To my amazing husband, my rock, and my biggest cheerleader. Your unwavering support and belief in me have been the foundation upon which I could build this dream. Thank you for being my biggest fan through every step of this process.

To my dear departed mother, whose voice I still hear encouraging me. You always taught me that I have it all within me and that I can be and do anything I put my mind to. This book honors the powerful seeds of confidence you planted in me.

To Business Network International, aka BNI, for teaching me the foundational principles of networking. Your frameworks gave me the structure I needed to step into leadership and learn to lead by example, proving that you build connection through intention and service.

To my incredible NLP coach and trainer, Stacey O'Byrne and her incredible wife, Marylou Hunter (MamaLou). You showed me how profoundly our mindset and state create our reality. The tools you taught me have directly shaped my personal and professional evolution.

To my fellow California Association of REALTORS Leadership Academy colleagues, thank you for consistently pushing me beyond the limits of what I thought I was capable of. Your ambition, drive, and camaraderie inspire me to always reach higher.

To AA, for teaching me the profound value of helping others selflessly. The lessons I learned have shaped my understanding of service and community in ways that extend far beyond the rooms.

To the many disappointments in local organized real estate, thank you for the invaluable lesson that *failure does not define me; it refines me.* These challenges were my greatest teachers, showing me the importance of learning from my own mistakes and turning setbacks into stepping stones.

To Coach K, for your powerful teachings on hyper-focus and managing distractions. Your wisdom helped me cut through the noise and dedicate myself to this work. This is just the beginning.

To my real estate and coaching clients, who have taught me something new with every interaction. It is an honor to be a part of your journey, and you continually inspire me with your growth and breakthroughs.

Finally, I am grateful for the journey of growth itself. It is the force that keeps me alive, engaged, and in love with this beautiful life. It truly is a good life.

Introduction

For years, I dreamed of writing a book but I constantly judged myself, asking, "Why me? Who would want to hear my story? Will my voice even matter?" These same questions hold many introverts back, especially when it comes to stepping into the world of networking.

I spent far too long believing the myth that my introverted nature was holding me back from real connection and success. Me, the same guy who can now lead a team, and speak in front of a room or on camera like it's no big deal. Like many introverts, I struggled with limiting beliefs and the myth that networking was for outgoing people. I quickly discovered the truth that we introverts have our own strengths that can take us far in our professional lives. That's why I'm writing this book. I want to help fellow introverts break through mental barriers and discover a way to network that reflects who they truly are.

I'm an introvert who used to feel like networking was just for extroverts. Everything that has to do with networking, like working a room, making small talk, and exuding confidence, can feel overwhelming, perhaps even impossible for introverts. But honestly, we are uniquely equipped to make deeper, more authentic connections. Yup, we really are! That's the sauce! Introversion is NOT a limitation. It's an asset for effective networking.

NETWORKING FOR INTROVERTS

This book is a guide to implementing networking and marketing strategies that align with who YOU are, allowing you to build relationships, grow your business, and achieve your goals, YOUR WAY. By leveraging your natural attributes, such as observation, listening, empathy, and thoughtfulness, you can create genuine relationships that become the foundation for your success.

What lies ahead isn't just a set of strategies but a candid reflection of a journey hard-won, marked by self-doubt, trial-and-error, and resilience. I'm inviting you to join me as I share not only the practical frameworks and tools that ultimately worked for me, but also the many stumbles, learning curves, and vulnerable moments of self-discovery I experienced along the way. Throughout these pages, you'll find stories and lessons that pull directly from my life. There's no sugar-coating, just hard lessons and honest reflections.

As you'll discover in Chapter 1, "Becoming the Networking Ninja," my origin story is one of intense hesitation—I was a master at self-sabotage before I ever became a master at networking. The internal battle between wanting to leave an impact and feeling unworthy of attention held me back far longer than any external obstacle. If you recognize a bit of yourself in that struggle, know this: You're not alone, and you do not have to take the long, painful road I did.

Through personal anecdotes, practical tools, and my most valuable frameworks like the SAFER Networking framework, this book will empower you to redefine what success looks like. Together, we'll challenge

INTRODUCTION

that majorly outdated belief that only the loudest voice wins.

I encourage you to use this book as a roadmap for navigating your entrepreneurial path with confidence and authenticity. Along the way, I'll reveal stories from my own transformation, like how I made the leap from IT business analyst to real estate entrepreneur, the major mindset shifts I made after professional setbacks, and the unexpected opportunities that came when I embraced vulnerability. You'll discover the building blocks of progress: how to ask for help, prioritize deep listening over shallow chatter, and find the courage to persist even when it's uncomfortable.

Whether you're striving to gain clients, expand your sphere of influence, or develop your leadership skills, the chapters ahead offer practical support with each turn. You'll get reflection prompts, actionable checklists, and the wisdom I've gained through mistakes and course corrections. We'll explore why your story matters and how authenticity attracts genuine connections and creates real progress.

You'll find the following pages divided into two sections: "Section I - The Work" and "Section II - Into Action." After most points in "The Work" section, there are reader reflection prompts. I STRONGLY encourage you to do the work. It will deepen the learning.

Please don't do what I did and follow the path of fear and avoidance that my insecurities created in my head. Instead, let my honest stories about setbacks and lessons help you leapfrog over obstacles that at one time

NETWORKING FOR INTROVERTS

seemed impossible. If you've ever felt invisible in a room full of extroverts, or let self-doubt silence your mojo, this book is here to help. It is meant to equip you for a life, and a network, built on your purpose and unique power.

Welcome to your new networking chapter. Let's begin!

Section I - The Work

This section is where we lay the foundation for your personal and professional growth. Consider this section as the starting point, the moment we hit the road. First, you'll get candid reflections of what I've learned through years of experience, trials, reflections, and of course, lots of mistakes along the way. It's about sharing the raw, authentic stories that shaped my understanding of purpose, or my "why," and discovering the systems that work for me when it comes to achieving success. Authenticity is the undercurrent here; it is prominent in both my stories and the lessons I weave throughout the chapters ahead.

Over the years, I've come to realize that, more than our wins, our greatest teachers are the missteps, the hard-won lessons, and the moments of doubt and uncertainty. These are the experiences that shape our character, refine our direction, and teach us what we're truly capable of when we stay committed to growth. I'll cover key insights in the chapters to come, like the importance of cultivating a resilient mindset, building powerful daily habits, mastering intentional goal-setting, and implementing useful frameworks like SIDE and RADICAL Focus. You'll learn how tools like focused reflection, stillness, and incremental change have become some of my most valuable superpowers for personal and professional growth.

This section will also dive into the art of networking—not just the surface-level kind, but the intentional, meaningful cultivation of relationships that can redefine your personal and professional life. You'll learn about the art of storytelling as a bridge to building authentic connections, and how to craft your narrative in a way that ensures you stand out with confidence. If you've ever felt unprepared or like you have your pants down in a room full of people, I'll show you how to use YOUR unique strengths to feel confident, shine, and make memorable impressions.

What sets this section apart is its focus on practical wisdom. It includes my tested strategies, tools, and systems that I built from a lifetime of observation, mistakes, experimentation, and feedback. Each lesson includes actionable steps: what actually works, why mindset is critical, and how to build a sustainable toolkit that keeps you moving forward at any stage of your journey.

I'll share stories that capture the messy reality of personal and professional development and the breakthroughs that followed. My intent in sharing these stories is that they will empower you, help you see that growth is rarely linear, and show you that the struggles you face today can make you stronger and more resilient.

You'll also get an in-depth look at how to align your goals with your values, to create a sense of purpose that drives every decision you make.

I hope you'll approach these pages not as a static checklist, but as a living, breathing guide that adapts and grows with you over time. The tools, frameworks, and words of encouragement you'll find here are ones I've relied on through every stage of my own journey and continue to use even now.

By sharing my story, I hope to inspire you to write and live your own way.

So let's dive in, get busy, and do the work. The journey is yours to shape, and I can't wait to see what you'll create.

Chapter 1: Becoming the Networking Ninja

Every great success story begins with an unexpected twist, a moment when the path ahead feels uncertain or impossible to find. For me, that moment came when life threw me into being a reluctant entrepreneur, a title I did not seek or was prepared for. Like many introverts, I never saw myself as a networker or leader. Not in a million years! I found peace and comfort in the structure of my IT career, where my introversion felt natural. But life, in its unpredictable way, had other plans.

The dot-com crash wasn't just a career-ending event; it was a catalyst for renewal. Forced to rethink my trajectory, I stumbled into real estate—first as a practical solution, and eventually as an entirely new chapter of my life. That transition was anything but smooth. I had to confront failure after failure, redefine how I viewed success, and build a foundation of confidence from the ground up. Most importantly, I discovered that my quieter strengths like observation, listening, and careful preparation weren't weaknesses. They were tools I needed to adapt in an industry dominated by extroversion. Or so I thought...

Networking, in particular, became both my greatest challenge and my greatest advantage. I learned that successful connections don't come from being the loudest voice in the room; they come from building relationships rooted in trust and authenticity. Over time, I developed systems and strategies to leverage my introversion not just to survive networking environments, but to excel in them. That's the heart of what I want to share with you now.

This chapter is about reframing how we approach connection and opportunity in networking. Whether you're navigating a new career path, creating a business, or building meaningful relationships, there are tools and mindsets that can transform how you show up in the world. You don't need to change who you are; you need to learn how to channel your unique strengths in a way that serves you and those around you. Because no matter where you are in your story, one fact remains true: Success is not about fitting into someone else's mold. It's about finding, and owning, your own way forward. Now, let's explore what that path can look like.

The Unexpected Path: From IT to Reluctant Entrepreneur

I never thought of myself as an extrovert. My upbringing shaped me into someone who was very shy, insecure, and, to be honest, deeply unsure of their worth. My self-esteem was fragile and I spent much of my earlier years in survival mode, never thinking further than the next step or challenge, like paying the rent or taking that trip back home. This mindset followed me well into adulthood. While I achieved important milestones, earning both a bachelor's and master's degree by the 1990s, I still lacked

CHAPTER 1: BECOMING THE NETWORKING NINJA

a compelling "why." My life was dictated by necessity, not by purpose or passion. It was easier to just stay afloat than to envision something more—more fulfillment, more meaning, and even more happiness.

By the early 2000s, I had carved out a solid career for myself in IT. I was good at what I did, and I loved my job. It gave me a sense of identity and accomplishment, something I hadn't often felt before. But life has a way of throwing curveballs. Right?! When the dot-com bubble burst, so too did that chapter of my career. I found myself unemployed in an industry that seemed to crumble overnight, with no clear career prospects. That loss hit me harder than I could have imagined, not just financially, but emotionally, mentally, and spiritually as well. My identity had been entirely tied to my role in IT, and without it, I felt completely lost. Who was I without my work? What value did I have in the world if not for what I could contribute professionally? The questions were gut-wrenching, and truthfully, I didn't have the answers.

At that time, I was also dabbling with the idea of real estate. It began as a practical solution to a family proposition; my partner suggested I pursue my broker's license to help us financially. It seemed like a logical backup plan while I searched for clarity in my life. With a master's degree and a little momentum, I arrogantly assumed that passing the state broker exam and establishing myself in the industry would all be a walk in the park.

How wrong I was.

 *"Success is not about fitting into someone else's mold. It's about finding, and owning, your own way."*

First, I underestimated the importance of preparation for the exam. Back then, there weren't countless online resources and streamlined guides. With little time left before the exam date, I realized I had to wade through books, seven of them, to be exact, and prepare like my life depended on it. And then, the unthinkable happened—on my first attempt, I failed.

I remember the devastation I felt getting that first result. I was used to success in academics and in my IT career, and failure wasn't something I encountered often. That first failure brought about an intense emotional reaction, anger, self-doubt, and frustration all rolled into one humiliating package. It hurt even more because it followed on the heels of losing that wonderful IT job. But somewhere in me, a voice nudged me forward. Maybe it was my perfectionism or stubbornness, maybe it was resilience I didn't know I had, or maybe it was simply my refusal to quit. It was most likely all of it!

I prepared more, focused harder, and built up my confidence before taking the exam a second time. Once again, I was met with failure, another rejection that stung even more deeply than the first. I started wondering if I was even cut out for it. My brain piled on the negative self-talk, flooding my thoughts with stories of how unprepared and unworthy I was. At some point, it all became too much, and I realized I couldn't do this on my own anymore. I needed to try something drastically different.

I knew the third time I took it would be my last shot, my Hail Mary. That's when I found a live, two-day prep course designed to prepare prospective real estate licensees not just for the knowledge portion of the exam but with a test-taking strategy. The class provided practical tips I hadn't considered. I learned that this was as much a reading comprehension test as it was a knowledge-based one. For example, those tiny words embedded in the questions, like "not," "nor," or "except," completely shift the meaning of a question. For the first time, I stopped relying purely on memorization and started approaching the exam with awareness and clarity.

Armed with these new tools, I walked into my third attempt feeling calm, empowered, and genuinely prepared. This time was different. I left the exam knowing I had given it my best, and finally, several weeks later, the results confirmed it. I passed. I officially earned my California real estate broker's license.

That milestone was a turning point not just because I achieved the credentials, but because of what I learned about myself along the way. For so long, I made decisions that protected my ego while also struggling with crippling self-doubt. The first two failures were a lesson in humility, a reminder that being "smart" or "qualified" wasn't enough. I had to be open to learning and asking for help when I fell short.

"Resilience isn't built in times of ease, but in the moments you choose to rise despite every reason to stay down."

You see, failing twice wasn't the end of my story; it was the foundation of my growth. I discovered a grit I didn't know I had, a resolve to keep going even when progress seemed impossible, and an understanding that setbacks are opportunities in disguise. What I once viewed as soul-crushing defeats became moments that led to transformation. They forced me to evaluate what I wanted out of my career and who I wanted to be as a person.

From there, my mindset shifted. With my broker's license in hand, I began carving out my place in the real estate industry. But more importantly, I started creating a life that reflected my values and passions. It wasn't easy and I made plenty of mistakes along the way, but for the first time, I was driven by something greater than survival. I was creating a future I could be proud of.

If there's one thing I hope you take from my story, it's this: Failure isn't fatal. It's not a sign of weakness, nor is it the end of your potential. Failure is a teacher, often bitter, sometimes brutal, but always one of the best. Whether you're standing at the precipice of a new career, enduring personal setbacks, or questioning your next step, know that every challenge you face is part of a larger story. You are still writing yours. Trust the process, trust yourself, and don't be afraid to stumble. Because

CHAPTER 1: BECOMING THE NETWORKING NINJA

every stumble brings you one step closer to finding your strength.

For me, failing that state broker's exam wasn't just a hurdle in my professional life; it was a redefining moment that shaped the person I am today. Failure doesn't define me, it refines me. Every step forward, every leap of faith, and every victory I've achieved since then reminds me of this truth: Resilience isn't built in times of ease, but in the moments you choose to rise despite every reason to stay down.

Reader Reflection: Reflect on a moment when life pushed you outside of your comfort zone. How did it impact your personal growth?

The Birth of the Bowtie Coach: How Bowties Became My Brand Identity

Okay, picture this: It's 2015 and after a few setbacks, an attempt to return to the world of being an employee (which didn't happen easily), and a period of deep reflection, I made the decision that was right for me—I was returning to entrepreneurship and real estate in the desert. But how would I stand out? I was determined to chart my next chapter with purpose and my goal was clear but daunting: I needed a personal brand.

My brand needed to be polished yet approachable, professional but still authentically "me." Something that people would remember.

At the time, I didn't know the answer, but I was committed to figuring it out. One thing was for sure: I wasn't going to blend into the sea of beige slacks and polo shirts that I so often saw in the real estate world. (Although if I'm honest, that was literally my uniform on most days.) My personal style was calling out for a facelift.

Then one day, inspiration came from where it so often does, a friend.

At an event, I saw my friend bright-eyed and buttoned-up in a ... bowtie. The idea struck like lightning: bowties! Yes! They screamed individuality while staying professional. They were nerdy, classic, quirky, and that resonated with me. It was exactly the vibe I wanted: sharp, fun, and approachable. I could just grab a couple and roll with it.

Easy, right? Wrong.

Finding bowties became my personal treasure hunt, with me scavenging every corner of store after store, rack after rack. It was exhausting but oddly thrilling.

But wearing the bowtie wasn't enough. Oh no, I had to learn to tie it myself and trust me, that wasn't pretty. Picture hours of practice in front of mirrors, fumbling clumsily, and shouting frustrated, "Why is THIS so @#$%ing hard?!" Eventually, I turned to YouTube (bless

CHAPTER 1: BECOMING THE NETWORKING NINJA

those nerdy creators), and came to a magical realization: Learning to tie a bowtie is exactly like tying shoelaces.

Boom. I finally mastered the knot, and with that, I found a new confidence.

It quickly became my signature. My desert-dapper fashion was alive and well: dress shirts, slacks and dressy shorts in the summer when the sun wasn't messing around, and of course, the pièce de résistance—a bowtie. Always bowties. Why? Because, frankly, showing up the way I wanted to mattered.

What I didn't expect was the impact it would have on others. People noticed. They commented. Clients, colleagues, and strangers connected with it. Somehow, a simple accessory had become a bridge to conversations, sparking curiosity and breaking the monotony of "safe" professional attire. At that point, I knew I was onto something. But creating a memorable look was only Step One; the next challenge was turning it into a cohesive tag line.

Cue one of the pivotal moments of my story. An offhand comment in a commercial real estate class changed everything. Imagine me, sitting there bowtied-up, when a classmate leans over and says, "Dude, you take the knots out of real estate." The words hit me like a ton of bricks. The metaphor was perfect. It wasn't just about the bowtie; it was about the "why," the service I offered my clients. I simplified what could be overwhelming for them. I tackled challenges, brought clarity, and made real estate easier. "That's it," I thought. That's my brand.

And so, that's when "Stephen Burchard: The Desert Bowtie Agent, Taking the (k)nots Out of Real Estate," came to life. It was clever, memorable, and exactly what I wanted. My tagline was more than a catchy slogan. It reflected everything I believed in: the idea that any seemingly impossible challenge could be unraveled with the right guidance (and a little confidence).

From there, my brand naturally evolved with my coaching spin-off. After all, my career extended far beyond real estate. Over 25 years, I'd faced the worst and best of entrepreneurship. It felt like the next logical step was to become the Bowtie Coach who "Takes the (k)nots Out of Business." I'd learned the values of clarity, adaptability, and, above all, persistence. Now, I wanted to pass those lessons on to others, helping them untangle whatever "knots" or limiting beliefs ("nots") were tripping them up in their professional or personal journeys. I'm sure you know these "knots" well: self-doubt, obstacles, and comments from the itty-bitty-shitty committee in your head.

What struck me most through this branding adventure was how collaborative it all was. The bowtie itself, the tagline, the metaphor—it didn't just come from me. It was my buddy unknowingly sparking the idea, my classmate helping me refine it, and even the countless YouTubers who set me on the knot-tying path. Finding inspiration wasn't a solo endeavor; it took a community to shape the Bowtie Agent, and eventually, the Bowtie Coach.

For me, the bowtie isn't just an accessory, and the tagline isn't just a slogan. Together, they've become symbols of resilience, creativity, and defying convention. They remind me, and hopefully others, that success isn't about fitting into anyone else's mold. It's about finding the courage to carve your own path while staying grounded in authenticity.

If you're staring down your own "branding battle" or facing seemingly impossible challenges, remember this: You may not figure it out all at once. Show up, trust the process, and never underestimate the power of one small decision to spark transformation. Sometimes, all it takes is a bowtie.

 *Reader Reflection*: Think of a seemingly small moment that shaped your personal brand or mission. Write about how it connects to your work today.

From Shy to Strategic: Leveraging Introversion

It's funny how life has a way of taking what you might initially view as a weakness and transforming it into one of your biggest strengths. Growing up, I was shy and insecure, cripplingly so. Speaking up in class or voicing my opinion in a group? Those weren't actions that came naturally to me. And while it may have seemed like these traits would only hold me back, I've realized that they gave me some of the greatest tools in my entrepreneurial toolbox today.

Being shy and insecure forced me to listen more—*really* listen. When you don't have the loudest voice in the room, you start to hear what isn't obvious. You notice the doubts tucked behind someone's confident tone, the unspoken ideas that hang in the air waiting to be voiced, the subtle patterns that reveal someone's true motivations or values. Listening wasn't just a way to cope with my shyness; it was how I learned to connect. And connection is an invaluable currency in the world of networking.

Listening helped me understand, and understanding helped me strategize. I soon realized that my quiet nature wasn't a shortcoming at all; it was my edge. While others were quick to jump into discussions or solutions, I often sat back and absorbed everything. Through observation, I discovered insights that others may have overlooked. Even in those early days of discomfort, I developed a skill that would serve me for years to come.

I leaned into my natural desire for solitude and reflection by immersing myself in research. I loved reading, summarizing, and simplifying complex ideas into something clear and actionable, for myself and for those around me. It was a coping mechanism but also an exercise in refinement. Without meaning to, I was training myself to zero in on what mattered most. By the time I found myself navigating the competitive and unpredictable world of real estate, I realized how powerful this ability was. Beyond selling homes, I was solving people's problems, helping them turn their visions into reality. My shyness had taught me how to listen to people's concerns, and my love for analysis had taught

CHAPTER 1: BECOMING THE NETWORKING NINJA

me how to prepare effectively so their worries could be replaced by confidence.

Of course, there were moments where my introversion still felt like a challenge. Networking events were daunting. Cold calls felt foreign. Being in a high-energy, extrovert-dominated industry made me feel like I had to adjust constantly, to fit into a mold that wasn't built for me. But I learned over time that fitting in often means diluting the very traits that make you valuable. Instead of trying to keep up with more outgoing personalities, I started doubling down on what I brought to the table. I redefined success on my own terms. Success didn't mean being the loudest in the room or overwhelming people with charisma. For me, success was about building trust, creating genuine relationships, and delivering consistent value to my clients.

"You don't need to change who you are. You need to learn how to channel your unique strengths in a way that serves you and those around you."

The transition wasn't immediate, nor was it easy. It took me months, then years, to unlearn the common narrative that being more outgoing was the way to achieve success. It took time for me to truly believe that my voice and my style of leadership had merit. Learning to leverage my introversion was about survival at first. But over time, it became something more intentional. As I grew, I began to see that my reflective, strategic approach was just as impactful as an outspoken one. I started recognizing that business and life thrive on diversity in every way, including diversity of thought, perspective, and personality.

My introversion gave me an edge in focusing on relationships over transactions. Whether it was with a friend, a mentor, or a client, I wasn't interested in surface-level exchanges. I wanted meaningful connections, and that desire resonated with the people I worked with. Someone who cares deeply, who listens first and acts decisively, stands out in a world where shallow noise often overshadows substance.

Through my personal and professional journey, I've realized there is no single formula for success, and not every solution begins with a loud, confident answer. Sometimes, progress starts with quiet observation, reflecting on possibilities, and finding the courage to break through in your own way. And sometimes, success feels slow because you're not taking the same path as others, but that doesn't make it any less significant.

If you are navigating the world with traits that feel at odds with traditional notions of success, I want to tell you this: You are not broken. You don't need to rewrite your personality to achieve greatness. Every personality, every strength, every perceived weakness has its place. It's about finding the systems, routines, and opportunities that fit *you*. Once I stopped trying to mirror external expectations and, instead, embrace the traits that make me feel most aligned with who I am, opportunities opened up in ways I couldn't have planned.

CHAPTER 1: BECOMING THE NETWORKING NINJA

I think back to those early days of shyness, when I was grappling with insecurity, and I see now how they formed the foundation for the entrepreneur I am today. Those moments of doubt taught me patience. The countless hours I spent observing taught me how to see others with empathy. The desire to overcome discomfort taught me resilience. Every piece of the puzzle, no matter how messy it looked at the time, has shaped the story I've built for myself.

There's immense power in being unapologetically yourself, in leaning into the quiet parts of you and showing up fully as you are. Your story matters just as much as anyone else's, and every step you take is an act of shaping that story. Trust in your unique way of navigating the world, in the choices you make that reflect your values, and trust that you are building resilience when things feel difficult.

 Reader Reflection: Write about a strength you've developed that began as a perceived weakness.

Building Quiet Confidence: Lessons In Networking and Development

Early in my entrepreneurial career, I was introduced to an organization called Business Network International (BNI). For an introvert looking to grow a business in what felt like an extrovert's industry, BNI was a revelation. It's a networking organization that operates on a system of structured frameworks and methodologies to facilitate referrals and professional growth. For someone like me, who thrives on having clear formulas and processes, this was a goldmine. BNI provided tools to build my business successfully, and it gave me a way to transform my insecurities into actionable strategies.

What's remarkable about the structure BNI provided is that it didn't rely on being the loudest voice in the room or the person who commanded all the attention. It valued relationship-building, thoughtfulness, and follow-through, traits that perfectly align with what I naturally bring to the table. By following the BNI frameworks, I was able to expand my real estate business and cultivate habits that continue to influence how I engage with clients and colleagues today. Formulas and structure became my safety nets, allowing me to step outside my comfort zone without feeling unanchored.

When I returned to real estate in the Coachella Valley in 2015, I knew I needed to leverage what I'd learned to reestablish myself. That's when I decided to create a new BNI chapter in the area, building it completely from scratch. Founding the chapter propelled my business forward and it showed me that systems can be extremely powerful in overcoming personal challenges. I used to think being shy was a limitation, but those years taught me that introversion and success are not mutually exclusive. By leaning into structured approaches to networking, I transformed what once felt like a burden into an asset.

My growth as an entrepreneur didn't stop there. My experiences in voluntary leadership took my

CHAPTER 1: BECOMING THE NETWORKING NINJA

understanding of the value of listening to an entirely new level. When I decided to invest my time in leadership positions with local boards, business organizations, and nonprofits, I didn't approach them with the intent of being front and center. Instead, I embraced my own unique contributions. Listening is one of the most important leadership skills, and I've found that true leadership also means hearing what others aren't saying, identifying opportunities, and bringing clarity to conversations.

One of my favorite responses when people ask why I don't speak up often in meetings or discussions is simple yet deeply rooted in who I am: "If I don't have something meaningful to add, why should I speak?" I've never believed in contributing for the sake of being heard. This mindset has shaped my role as a collaborator and a leader. It's not about being the loudest voice in the room; it's about ensuring that when I do speak, it carries weight and intention.

Another unexpected benefit of these leadership roles has been the knowledge and confidence I've gained—priceless assets that extend far beyond the boardroom. Interacting with influential leaders, understanding governance, and being part of crucial decisions at the local, state, and national levels have sharpened my skills and empowered me in ways I couldn't have imagined. This confidence spills over into how I engage with clients and colleagues. They see it in how I carry myself; I'm calm, informed, and confident. It's the kind of confidence that grows when you know your strengths, and you actively choose to lean into them.

"Every quiet observation, every thoughtful decision, every step you take is a part of the extraordinary life you are building."

I've come to understand over the years that authenticity is a kind of magnet. People want to work with individuals who are honest about who they are and what they bring to the table. By recognizing and leaning into my introverted strengths instead of trying to suppress them, I've been able to build deeper, more meaningful connections with my clients and colleagues. These connections aren't just about networking or business; they grow from trust and understanding, fundamental elements of any lasting professional relationship.

Looking back, every twist and turn in my career has further demonstrated to me that introversion is an asset, not a hindrance. From carefully listening and understanding what's truly needed in any conversation to building entire chapters of thriving BNI networks and meaningfully contributing to the growth of organizations in my role as a board member, my quiet nature has been the secret ingredient to my success. For every insecurity I've felt, there's been a tool or strategy to guide me through. For every challenge I've faced, there's been an opportunity to transform a perceived flaw into a feature.

To thrive professionally as an introvert, you don't need to eliminate weaknesses; you need to find ways to turn your natural attributes into strengths while staying rooted in authenticity. My shyness taught me how to

CHAPTER 1: BECOMING THE NETWORKING NINJA

listen, my insecurities taught me how to analyze and prepare, and my introversion overall taught me the value of depth instead of staying on the surface. Every step has reinforced the importance of trusting the process, showing up, and leaning into what makes me unique.

If you see yourself in these words, I want you to know this: You are not at a disadvantage because of how you're wired. You don't need to force yourself to be someone you're not to succeed. Find the systems, structures, and frameworks that work for you. Seek opportunities to turn your perceived weaknesses into your unique advantages. And most importantly, every decision you make, no matter how small, has the power to shape your story into something extraordinary. Your voice, your talents, and your way of navigating the world have value. Trust in that. Trust in yourself.

 Reader Reflection: Imagine explaining the "aha moments" from your networking and leadership experiences to a fellow introvert starting their own journey. Record it in your journal.

I encourage you to think for a moment about the challenges you've faced in your own life, the moments that felt impossible or the times you doubted your path. Now, consider how you overcame them. Every time you navigated those difficult waters, you built strength, resilience, and character. You taught yourself how to adapt, even if it didn't feel like it at the time. Those are the moments that define you, and they're also the moments you can lean on when the next challenge arises.

There is power in reflection, in recognizing the patterns in your past and seeing how they've contributed to your growth over time. Sometimes, it's the moments of chaos, doubt, and uncertainty that teach us the most about ourselves.

Growth isn't about a single breakthrough or monumental achievement. It's about small, intentional actions over time that lead to transformation. It's about choosing to show up every day, whether it's easy or difficult, and holding onto a belief that you are moving toward something meaningful—even if it's not entirely clear what that is yet. Your story is unfolding. Every quiet observation, every thoughtful decision, every step you take helps build the extraordinary life and career ahead of you.

Chapter 2: The Strengths of Introversion

When the next challenge arises, it may feel overwhelming, but remember there is power in reflection. Taking a step back to look at the patterns in your past allows you to see how the most unexpected moments, chaotic, doubt-filled, or uncertain, have shaped you. They sure have shaped me! These weren't just setbacks or obstacles; they were opportunities for clarity and growth. The truth is, some of the hardest parts of life help shape your unique perspective and build inner strength. For a long time, I didn't see it that way.

I used to believe that being an introvert was a weakness. Everywhere I turned, society seemed to favor traits that didn't come naturally to me. People praised outgoing personalities, charismatic leaders dominated social settings, and those loud, confident voices seemed to overshadow quieter ones. I felt like I didn't belong. I bought into the myths about introverts, that we were shy, antisocial, and unfit for leadership. I saw my need for solitude, my reflective nature, and my preference for meaningful conversations over small talk as barriers.

What I've come to learn is that being an introvert is not a liability. It's a superpower. Yes, I said superpower!

Introvert Superpowers

As introverts, we possess the awesome superpower of the ability for deep, focused thinking. While others might rush into decisions, striving to stay in the relentless flow of action, introverts often retreat into silence to think deeply and intentionally. This ability to step back and analyze allows us to uncover insights that others might miss. It fuels creativity, informs strategic decisions, and leads to moments of clarity that can transform our personal and professional lives.

I didn't always value this about myself. Early in my entrepreneurial journey, I thought I needed to always be out there connecting with everyone, attending all the events, and projecting nonstop energy. I quickly exhausted myself trying to meet those expectations, being someone I wasn't. Over time, I began to lean into my strengths. I carved out time for solitude, where I could reflect on my goals and map out my next steps with purpose. This was a game-changer, and it was the foundation I built everything else on.

Another remarkable trait of introverts is our ability to listen—not just to hear words but to truly understand. Active listening is our gateway to forming authentic, meaningful connections. While others may be quick to respond, focusing on what they'll say next, introverts create space for others to feel heard. This gift is invaluable, especially when building relationships in business or our personal lives. When people feel understood, trust and connection come easily.

CHAPTER 2: THE STRENGTHS OF INTROVERSION

Through empathetic listening, I began to unlock doors I didn't think were available to me. Doors to partnerships, collaborations, and mentorships that felt real and aligned with my values. We build the strongest relationships on mutual understanding and honesty, not surface-level banter.

Over time, I also started to realize my need for solitude wasn't something I needed to "fix." It was a strength. Solitude wasn't isolation, it was a tool for rejuvenation, creativity, and resetting. It allowed me to show up in the world as my best self. I began to see and believe that the real magic happened in the quiet.

Solitude and reflection helped me create and refine my vision with clarity. It was in those quiet times that I clarified my values, set my intentions, and examined what truly mattered to me. When I emerged, I engaged with the world more authentically, with confidence and clarity.

This understanding wasn't sudden or linear. It was a process of unlearning the myths I had internalized about who I was supposed to be and rewriting the narrative for myself. Slowly, over time, I stepped away from insecurities and shyness and leaned into focused, deep work and authentic connection.

 "Being an introvert is not a liability. It's a superpower! Solitude isn't isolation—it's a tool."

NETWORKING FOR INTROVERTS

What once felt like walls trapping me in my introversion turned out to be bridges to the kind of life I wanted to build.

One of the most underrated superpowers of introverts is our natural ability for empathy, the ability to sense the emotions, energy, and unspoken words of others. For us, connecting doesn't always happen through surface-level interactions. Instead, it happens when we tune into the subtler rhythms of human behavior.

Empathy has played a key role in my ability to network and foster relationships. When I stopped trying to project an image that didn't feel authentic to me and instead focused on being present, I began to see how much of an asset my empathetic nature could be. People value someone who genuinely sees them, someone who reaches into the heart of their story and meets them in their struggles and their dreams.

This kind of connection makes collaboration more meaningful and impactful.

Introvert superpowers, like deep thinking, listening, empathy, and the ability to connect authentically, are not traits we should be diminishing. They are strengths waiting to be harnessed, refined, and applied to your life's mission. Sometimes, the world may still feel like it's designed for the extroverted. But you can thrive on your own terms when you learn to lean into what makes you unique.

Introverted qualities are assets in entrepreneurship and networking because they create their own kind

CHAPTER 2: THE STRENGTHS OF INTROVERSION

of impact, one that is thoughtful, deliberate, and long-lasting. Whether we're brainstorming a new project in solitude, offering a listening ear at a critical moment, or building trust with an empathetic heart, these actions contribute to our success and the success of those around us.

It's not about meeting society's expectations. It's about showing up as we are, honoring the value we bring, and trusting that our unique way of navigating the world is enough. That's where true power lies, in being confident in our abilities. The quiet strength of introverts isn't just revolutionary—it's unstoppable. Remember, growth doesn't always come with fireworks or loud statements.

Reader Reflection: List three traits you once saw as challenges but are now your greatest assets as an introvert.

Harnessing Energy

Energy is an invaluable resource, one that shapes how we show up in the world and how we feel within. Learning to manage energy before, during, and after interactions has been a game-changer in my personal and professional life. For years, I had a habit of pouring myself into everything, burning the candle at both ends without realizing the toll it was taking. It wasn't until I started tuning into my habits and recognizing where my energy was slipping away that I discovered a healthier, more sustainable way to show up fully, for myself and others.

Now, I start each day with intentionality. Mornings set the tone, and I've learned that *mindset is the foundation of everything I do*. Before I engage with the outside world, before emails, meetings, or even small talk, I begin with practices that center me and prepare me for whatever comes my way. Meditation helps me quiet the noise and tune into what really matters. Prayer and gratitude shift my focus to abundance and possibility rather than lack or limitation. These moments of stillness and appreciation connect me to a higher sense of purpose, and it's from this grounded place that I can truly engage my best self for the rest of the day.

Ending the day is just as critical as starting it. My evenings are also sacred time, a chance to create, stretch my mind, and reflect. I turn to reading to inspire new thoughts, and journaling and meditation to process and release the events of the day. These practices aren't simply routines; they are vital acts of renewal, allowing my mind and body to recharge and my creativity to flow more freely. Through this reflection, I align myself with my goals and with a clearer, deeper sense of why I do what I do.

Of course, days are rarely symmetrical. Some are packed with activities like meetings, deadlines, and events, while others allow for more stillness and reflection. What I've come to understand is that finding balance doesn't mean every day should follow the same script. Instead, it's about listening closely to what I need in the moment. On busier days, it's crucial for me to carve out

CHAPTER 2: THE STRENGTHS OF INTROVERSION

space to recharge, perhaps with a mindful pause, some deep breathing, or even stepping outside for a short walk. Slowing down for just a few minutes can create enough space for me to refuel and prevent burnout.

On quieter days, I lean into reflection and renewal. These are the times for deeper reflection or pouring energy into something creative, without rushing or forcing outcomes. Interestingly, these slower moments are often just as productive, if not more, than packed schedules. They allow me to connect with ideas and insights that might otherwise get lost in the noise.

One of the most profound lessons I've learned is how much energy is freed up when I allow myself to be fully authentic. For years, I carried the weight of perfectionism, believing that I had to show up as an ideal version of myself. I layered on masks and walls, feeling the pressure to be "on" all the time, to perform, and to meet everyone else's expectations. Those barriers were exhausting, draining me faster than anything else.

 "Stop trying to conform to the expectations of an extroverted world. Lean into your natural tendencies by reflecting on your goals during quiet moments and then engaging intentionally."

Through years of trial and error, I realized that the more I embraced my true self, the less energy I needed to give toward "keeping up appearances." That's because authenticity is liberating. When I give myself permission to be fully present and unapologetically me, I don't just feel lighter—I feel stronger. My ideas flow more freely, my interactions hold more meaning, and my energy stretches further, fueling me in ways I didn't think were possible.

This doesn't mean that every day is perfect or that I'm immune to self-doubt. But I know now that building trust with myself, honoring who I am and what I bring, is the foundation for empowering myself and the relationships and opportunities that flow into my life.

Self-care is often misunderstood as something selfish and indulgent, but I've come to see it as vital to success. Exercise, eating well, and constantly learning have become non-negotiables in my life, for my health and my growth as an entrepreneur. When I invest in myself physically, mentally, and emotionally, I show up more effectively in every role.

The greatest lesson to take from this is the importance of adaptability. What we need today might not match what we needed yesterday or will need tomorrow. Some days, self-care means high-energy workouts or tackling challenging tasks head-on. Other days, it's prioritizing rest or giving ourselves permission to slow down. Instead of rigidly adhering to routines, I've learned to tune in to what is needed for the moment.

Energy management has taught me to move through my days, whether chaotic or calm, with a sense of flow rather than resistance. Resistance burns energy. Flow harnesses it. Learning how to acknowledge

CHAPTER 2: THE STRENGTHS OF INTROVERSION

what's happening and respond with grace rather than frustration has been one of the most empowering shifts in my mindset.

I've also found that managing interactions thoughtfully is essential. Whether it's a one-on-one conversation or speaking to a crowd, I now approach interactions with an awareness of energy exchange. Not every moment requires the same level of engagement, and not every person or situation deserves my full bandwidth. Being present doesn't mean overextending—it means being intentional with how and where I channel my focus.

The road to managing my energy and mindset effectively hasn't been easy. It required years of falling short, learning, and evolving. But every step helped me get to this understanding of balance and purpose. I've found a deeper truth: It's not about reaching some perfect end state. It's about showing up every day authentically, taking small, steady steps, and trusting the process.

Growth takes patience and self-compassion. The more we honor our needs and build systems that support us, the more we'll discover extraordinary possibilities.

As I continue this process, one thing remains clear—this is a lifelong evolution, and one worth committing to.

And when we take care of ourselves at the core, everything else becomes easier. Instead of pushing uphill with depleted momentum, we can meet our goals faster when we move with greater ease and intention.

Reader Reflection: Describe your ideal environment for recharging and how it helps fuel your work.

Redefining Networking

You don't have to adopt traditional, extrovert-centric methods to succeed in networking. Instead, lean into your natural strengths, like reflection, deep thinking, and an ability to foster connections, to carve your own path. Networking doesn't mean flitting from one contact to the next or collecting stacks of business cards. It means building quality relationships over time.

Ivan Misner, known as the father of modern networking, founder of BNI and bestselling author, has stated repeatedly, "Networking is a marathon, not a sprint." This has profound implications for introverts. This long-term approach allows you to be intentional about how you spend your energy and who you connect with. Success in networking is measured by how authentically you nurture your circle, not how quickly you expand it. Realizing this truth transformed how I approached professional interactions. Rather than pushing myself to match the pace of others, I learned to honor my own rhythm, and that made all the difference.

One of the most empowering lessons I've learned is to seek out quality over quantity when it comes to connections. It's easy to feel overwhelmed by the

CHAPTER 2: THE STRENGTHS OF INTROVERSION

pressure of networking events, where the sheer number of attendees might have you questioning whether you need to meet as many people as possible. You don't. It's perfectly okay to focus your energy on fostering one or two meaningful connections during an event.

Start small. Identify one or two individuals who pique your interest for a genuine conversation. Sometimes, that's all it takes to create a meaningful professional relationship. Skip the surface-level chatter and lean into the conversations that matter. Ask questions that reveal shared values or interests, those deeper threads that nurture long-term connections.

Large networking events can feel especially exhausting for introverts, but there's usually an opportunity to engage in smaller, more manageable groups. Look for a table or cluster where, ideally, you already know at least one person. Familiar faces can help you feel grounded, but they can also facilitate introductions to others in the group.

These small group settings are powerful because they allow for more natural and comfortable exchanges. The pressure to keep the dialogue alive doesn't rest on one person alone, and you'll likely find opportunities to contribute thoughtfully rather than feeling hurried or called out.

When possible, attend events with someone you trust and feel safe around. This wingperson can help ease the apprehension that often comes with stepping into a room full of unfamiliar faces. Whether it's a colleague or a friend, this shared experience can make navigating the event less intimidating. Plus, having a steady presence by your side can encourage you to push through moments of hesitation or discomfort.

However, I encourage you to not rely solely on this strategy. Use your wingperson as a source of support, but don't hesitate to step outside your comfort zone. You might surprise yourself with how capable you are of making solo connections once you feel more at ease.

Being in a high-energy networking environment can deplete an introvert's reserves quickly. That's why it's essential to strategize ways to protect your energy. Pay attention to where your boundaries are and don't be afraid to take a step back when you need to. Step outside for fresh air, duck into the bathroom for a moment of quiet, or relocate to a less crowded corner of the venue.

Remember, breaks aren't just acceptable; sometimes they're necessary. They help you recenter, recharge, and reapproach conversations with a clearer mind. Giving yourself permission to pause during an event doesn't mean you're failing or disengaging—it means you're prioritizing sustainability over burnout.

It can often feel like you're expected to stay the entire duration of a networking event. Here's the truth: You don't have to stay until the doors friggin' close. It's better to aim for quality engagement over endurance. Make sure you've had meaningful dialogue with a few people, then if you're toast and at your limit, it's okay to leave. It's better to walk away having made a few lasting impressions than to exhaust yourself in the pursuit of more.

CHAPTER 2: THE STRENGTHS OF INTROVERSION

The art of networking doesn't end when an event ends. True connections flourish in the follow-up. For introverts, meaningful follow-ups can be a sweet spot of networking. Instead of being lost in the shuffle of a busy room, you can dedicate time to personalized notes, emails, or messages that express genuine appreciation for the conversation you shared.

"Send handwritten notes or take time to highlight others' achievements. It's these small, thoughtful gestures that leave the biggest impact."

Follow-ups are about continuing the conversation and showing real interest, not keeping up appearances. A simple gesture like mentioning a specific topic or insight discussed during your interaction demonstrates attentiveness and leaves a lasting impression.

Networking as an introvert is less about adjusting who you are and more about creating systems and habits that align with your preferences and strengths. For instance, consider scheduling networking engagements in a way that gives you ample time to recharge between events. Virtual networking might also be a valuable alternative, as it allows for meaningful exchanges without the sensory overload of in-person gatherings.

Be intentional about which events or opportunities you pursue. Ask yourself how they align with your goals, energy levels, and values. You don't have to say yes to everything. Professional success is not about being everywhere; it's about being purposeful in where you choose to show up.

Every small, strategic step you take builds a foundation for long-term success, whether it's making a single connection at a time, taking a pause when necessary, or crafting thoughtful follow-ups. Networking is a long game, and introverts are perfectly suited to play it because of our ability to combine consistency, thoughtfulness, and authenticity.

Your approach may look different, and that's okay. By redefining the rules of networking, you're showing up for yourself and demonstrating to others that genuine connection always outlasts forced interaction.

Each moment you invest in sharing your authentic self and actively listening to others creates ripples that extend far beyond any single interaction. You have the capacity to nurture a network that matters—a network built on trust, understanding, and shared purpose. And that is the essence of success.

 Reader Reflection: Envision a networking experience tailored for introverts. What does it feel like?

We just dove deep into the misconceptions and surprising advantages of introversion. Now that we've uncovered the strengths of introversion and how it can

CHAPTER 2: THE STRENGTHS OF INTROVERSION

be an asset, we move to the next essential component of connection: developing a strong networking mindset.

Networking isn't just about meeting people; it's about nurturing meaningful connections that stand the test of time. The next chapter will guide you through my foundational principles that are necessary to approach networking with intentionality, authenticity, and purpose. By focusing on the value you bring and the relationships you build, you'll learn to redefine networking into a process that aligns with your professional goals and your growth as well. Together, we'll explore the mindset shift that helps introverts and especially helped me thrive in the art of connection.

Chapter 3: Foundations of a Networking Mindset

I've learned that every successful venture, whether personal or professional, begins with a strong foundation. While many see networking as simply a tool to achieve success, for closing deals, securing promotions, or building professional relationships, it is, at its core, a deeply personal endeavor. It demands self-awareness, inner clarity, and resilience. Throughout my life, I've dealt with challenges like anxiety, depression, and addiction, and the ability to connect authentically with others did not come naturally or easily to me. It was something I intentionally cultivated through struggle, growth, and an unrelenting commitment to improving my mindset.

> "Every great relationship requires presence, inner clarity, and resilience, a strong foundation for personal and professional growth."

The Power of Stillness and Focus

I can attribute much of my transformation to an essential realization: Working on being present, developing a mindfulness mindset, and refining my focus were the keys to not just surviving, but thriving. I began to grow through the power of stillness, the freedom in removing distractions, and the grounding power of exercise. These pillars laid the groundwork for what I call my SIDE framework, which actively supports my mindset and my approach to personal and professional relationships. This framework is a way for me to remember what's important to me.

The SIDE framework, which stands for "Stillness, Inputs, Distractions, and Exercise," consists of interconnected, mutually reinforcing elements. Together, they create a holistic system that fosters emotional clarity, mental strength, and a sense of purpose—for networking and for living a life that aligns with your values and aspirations.

1. Stillness

We live in a constant state of motion; our days are filled with endless notifications, tasks, and pressures. This external chaos often mirrors our minds, creating anxiety and depleting our emotional reserves. Early in my personal growth, I discovered the power of stillness. While the idea of slowing down seemed counterintuitive, especially with so many goals to chase, I realized that I needed to take intentional moments to pause in order to regain focus and perspective.

Stilling the mind doesn't always mean sitting in perfect stillness, meditating cross-legged on a yoga mat (though meditation is undoubtedly helpful if it works for you). It means learning to pause and redirect your thoughts when things feel overwhelming. For me, this came through simple practices like deep breathing exercises, journaling my thoughts without judgment, and carving out uninterrupted time to reflect.

It requires small, actionable steps. Start by identifying when your mind feels chaotic, when stress or negativity is at its peak. Pay attention to your triggers. Then, disrupt the pattern with a pause. Take a few deep breaths, reflect, and assess what action truly aligns with your purpose. Over time, you'll build mental muscles that help you approach challenges with calm confidence.

2. Inputs

In the world today, we are always taking in a constant barrage of information. Whether it's from social media, the news, or the relentless noise of ads, it all shapes how we think, feel, and act. Unfortunately, not all inputs are constructive. I realized I was consuming material and exposing myself to environments that fed my anxiety and caused me to feel insecure and rattled. I was absorbing the negativity around me without questioning its impact. Oops!

By becoming intentional with what I allowed into my life, I took back control. This meant unfollowing accounts that always left me feeling inferior, choosing books that made me feel inspired and empowered instead of drained, and seeking conversations that made me feel uplifted. I asked myself a simple but profound question whenever I allowed something to enter my mental space: "Is this helping me grow, or is it in my way?"

This practice is about carefully curating positive influences. Seek out mentors through their writings, videos, and in-person interactions. Surround yourself with people who embody the values you aspire to adopt. Remember, your mind is like a sponge; make sure it's absorbing energy and material that serves your growth rather than undermines it.

 "Your mind is like a sponge; make sure it's absorbing energy and material that serves your growth rather than undermines it."

---

3. Distractions

Distractions come in many forms, like your smartphone or computer buzzing every few minutes with notifications. Emails, a relentless to-do list, or even an overactive mind can make you resist focusing on the present task. For years, I allowed distractions to define my day. I was "busy," but I wasn't moving toward my goals. One of the most liberating lessons I learned was just how important it is to eliminate distractions! What a Godsend!

This begins with a simple acknowledgment: *Not everything deserves our attention.* To dispel distractions, you need clarity about what matters most to you. Set your priorities at the start of the day, then design your

CHAPTER 3: FOUNDATIONS OF A NETWORKING MINDSET

environment to support those priorities. For example, if you're focused on building meaningful connections, put your phone away during conversations. Duh! If accomplishing a task requires focus, block off specific times to work and communicate your boundaries to those around you.

Removing distractions is about being intentional, not achieving perfection. Forgive yourself when you get off course, but always come back to the question, "Is this distraction worth the time it's taking away from my focus?"

4. Exercise

Of all the mindset tools I've learned to prioritize, exercise has been one of the most supportive. Early in my life, I didn't fully understand the mind-body connection. I discovered over time that physical movement isn't just about aesthetics or fitness; it's a vehicle for mental clarity, emotional regulation, and increased energy. Woohoo!

Regular exercise releases endorphins, the brain's natural "feel-good" chemicals. It also builds physical resilience that mirrors mental strength. Whether it's a brisk walk outdoors, yoga, weightlifting, or swimming, exercise is a powerful reminder of what your body and mind can achieve when they work together.

For me, exercise became a bridge between my inner and outer worlds. A brisk morning walk helped me release negativity and begin the day with a clear head. Even short midday walks and stretches kept me centered during moments of stress. The key is finding what movement works and committing to it as a non-negotiable part of your routine.

When you integrate these four elements, stilling the mind, limiting inputs, dispelling distractions, and exercising, you create a powerful system for rewriting and supporting your mindset, so you can grow intentionally. You don't have to be perfect in all four areas or be able to juggle them simultaneously. (Good luck with that!) Instead, it's about finding your unique way forward, assessing what you need in the moment, and building a strong mindset over time.

The SIDE framework is a philosophy. It teaches you that by focusing inward with clarity and purpose, you can transform how you connect with others and how you live your life. With this foundation in place, you'll find that networking, like so many things, becomes easier and more fulfilling.

The first step is understanding the power of your own mind and its ability to create the future you envision. With SIDE as a mindset guide, you will have a foundation that helps you face life's challenges and transform your personal and professional world. Start now, one step, one pause, one choice at a time, and you will have everything you need to succeed.

CHAPTER 3: FOUNDATIONS OF A NETWORKING MINDSET

 Reader Reflection: Write about a recent moment when you embraced stillness. What small steps can you take to expand or strengthen your stillness practices?

RADICAL Focus

Only in the last few years have I truly understood the power of focus and how it transforms my ability to move ahead productively and with more purpose. That realization didn't come overnight; it came through a blend of frustration, experimentation, and a burning desire to stop spinning my wheels. I needed a game plan, something actionable and repeatable, to keep me grounded and directed. That's when I created my RADICAL Focus framework. This strategic approach skyrocketed my productivity, transformed how I work, and helped me create measurable progress toward both my professional and personal goals. It's simple and effective.

RADICAL Focus is a mindset shift. It's about stripping away distractions, staying present, and doing the right things at the right time to create momentum. Each part of the framework works in harmony with the others, empowering you to focus on what matters most while tuning out the noise. Let's break it down:

1. Remember Your Why

For much of my life, I didn't feel like I had a compelling "why." I wasn't driven by kids or family commitments, and I often told myself I had all the time in the world to accomplish everything I wanted. That illusion of infinite time led me to squander opportunities and procrastinate on creating the future I knew deep down I wanted.

At the heart of focus lies a clear, compelling "why." When you know why you're doing something, it becomes easier to push through challenges, resist distractions, and maintain your motivation. Write your "why" down, and keep it somewhere visible, like on your desk, in your planner, or even as your phone's lock screen. This constant reminder keeps it front and center, helping you align your daily actions with your long-term vision. And it's okay if your "why" evolves. Life changes and your purpose and motivation should grow with you.

2. Add Time Blocks

Time blocking was foreign to me and I resisted it like the plague. I already had a full schedule so dividing my calendar into specific blocks of time seemed counterintuitive and stupid. However, I saw the gold value in using calendar boundaries to protect my time and energy, so I needed to reframe it in my mind. I decided to see it as creating an ideal calendar.

Time blocking is a powerful technique for managing your days intentionally. By allocating specific

CHAPTER 3: FOUNDATIONS OF A NETWORKING MINDSET

blocks of time to focus on important tasks, you set clear boundaries and create a structure that supports deep work. Honor your time blocks as sacred. These are promises you make to yourself and, more importantly, they are necessary to meet your goals. During these focus sessions, turn off all distractions, communicate your availability, or lack thereof, to others, and commit fully to the task at hand. You'll be amazed at how much clarity and progress you can generate when you're working intentionally, without distractions.

3. Delete Notifications

This was a HUGE game changer for me: removing those nasty pings, dings and other notifications that kept coming up on my phone, watch, tablet, and computer. They pulled my focus away from what I was doing and after, it took me a bit of time to get back into my groove. I didn't realize how much they affected me until I turned them off. Taadaa!

Notifications are an enemy to focus. Every ping, buzz, and badge pulls you out of the zone and disrupts your momentum. Be ruthless about eliminating them. For real! Turn off email alerts, social media notifications, and app badges. The only notifications I allow during my focus time are communications with my team, clients, and family. Remember, your attention is one of your most valuable resources—guard it fiercely.

4. Insulate Your Environment

When I started to use Focus time on my phone, this altered my availability significantly. It allowed me to focus better and remove distractions that eroded my productivity and interrupted my time with clients and colleagues. However, if there are important connections and conversations I don't want to miss, I make sure to tell people how to connect with me despite my Focus filters.

Your environment can either support or undermine your efforts to focus. Take control by creating a space free of unnecessary noise and distractions. Close your email, put your phone on "Do Not Disturb," and make your workspace conducive to productivity. Insulating your environment isn't just about physical space; it's also about setting mental boundaries, letting go of multitasking, and being fully present in the moment.

"Set daily priorities and create an environment free from distractions—turn off notifications to focus deeply on building meaningful connections."

5. Choose One Thing

I used to think multitasking allowed me to get more done. Well, multitasking simply doesn't work. When I tried it, my mind was fractured and it sucked my focus away big time. I was making tiny steps of progress on a lot of things, but when I stopped trying to multitask, I started making big leaps on priority tasks.

Multitasking is a myth when it comes to productivity. Your brain works best when it focuses on one thing at a time. Choose the most important task, and commit to it fully until it's completed or when you reach a natural stopping point. By simplifying your focus, you'll gain clarity, reduce stress, and produce higher-quality results. The truth is, trying to do everything at once often leads to doing nothing well.

6. Accountability

I have accomplished much more in my life than I thought possible by having accountability partners for my business tasks and goals. Knowing I have someone to check in with prompts me to take action and complete what I said I would. They also push me to do more than I would on my own!

Accountability is a powerful motivator. Share your goals with someone you trust, who will encourage you to stay on track. This could be a coach, mentor, friend, or colleague. External accountability keeps you aligned with your commitments and helps you push through when your motivation wanes. Regularly check in with your accountability partner to review progress and recalibrate if needed.

7. Limit Your Availability

Limiting my availability was difficult at first. I thought I had to be available to those around me 24/7, and then at the end of the day, I'd be pissed I didn't accomplish what I set out to do. This is similar to using Focus time, however, this is more about the people around us in our offices or homes. We get asked, "Have you got a minute?" all the time, right? Well, is it ever just a minute? Nooooope!

Every interruption dilutes your focus, so limiting your availability during deep work sessions is crucial. Communicate clear boundaries to those around you, whether it's teammates, clients, or family, and set expectations about when and how you'll be accessible. I only check my email two to three times a day, and during focus time, I only select a few people who can reach me. These boundaries aren't just about protecting your time; they're about respecting your goals and priorities.

RADICAL Focus is a roadmap, one you can adapt and personalize to suit your needs. The key to getting where you want to be is to approach your goals with intention, clarity, and purpose. With each small step forward, you're building momentum—and with momentum comes transformation. Take one step today, no matter how small, toward aligning your actions with your ideal vision. You already have everything you need within you to succeed. When you focus, act, and keep your "why" at the center, the life you envision is within reach.

CHAPTER 3: FOUNDATIONS OF A NETWORKING MINDSET

 *Reader Reflection*: Imagine explaining your "why" to a close friend. How would you tell that story?

Building a Growth Mindset

To focus your mindset on growth, first start with accepting that growth is not a destination. It's a constant evolution, one that requires accountability, self-awareness, and resilience. This mindset is cultivated day by day through intentional actions and a commitment to personal and professional development. There were moments in my life when setbacks felt insurmountable, struggles shook my confidence, and mistakes left me feeling stuck. But over time, I discovered something empowering: I had the ability to own my failures, reflect on my missteps, and emerge stronger than before. This shift wasn't easy but it changed everything, propelling me toward a life filled with meaning and progress.

When I was younger, I often thought about my personal and spiritual growth. I sought fulfillment through reflection, connection, and learning. I was driven by a deep desire to improve myself, not because I felt unworthy but because I believed there was always more to uncover, more to develop within me, more ways to contribute. I believed this to be true because every time I leaned into growth, my life gained momentum. I experienced opportunities that I may not have had if I had clung to old patterns or excuses. Growth exhilarated me. I saw my life expand with every new skill, insight, and perspective I acquired.

However, this process required me to shed a victim mindset that I, at times, unconsciously carried. It's easy to fall into the trap of blaming circumstances on others, letting external forces dictate your state of mind and life trajectory. But here's the truth I learned through trial and error: Accountability is freedom. It's about taking full ownership of your choices and understanding that, while you can't always control what happens to you, you can control how you respond. No matter the defeat or disappointment, when I make the choice to be accountable, I reclaim my power and move with greater clarity and purpose.

To fuel my growth, I turn to books, surrounding myself with words of wisdom and knowledge that expand my thinking. I engage in conversations with individuals who challenge and encourage me. I seek out environments where learning is a priority, whether through education, professional training, or informal connections. These habits aren't optional; they have become non-negotiable practices in my life. They have been the building blocks that have equipped me with the tools to keep learning, stay curious, and evolve.

 "Growth isn't about perfection. It's about showing up with an attitude that prioritizes alignment with your goals and values."

CHAPTER 3: FOUNDATIONS OF A NETWORKING MINDSET

My professional growth began to take shape during my undergraduate and graduate studies in business, sharpening my understanding of strategy, leadership, and innovation. From there, my passion for real estate inspired me to earn my broker's license. Later, I immersed myself in the field of neuro-linguistic programming (NLP), an approach to personal development that connects thoughts, language, and behavioral patterns to help people achieve their goals. I received extensive training and became a Certified NLP Trainer, which allowed me to build a strong foundation in coaching and mentoring techniques. Each of these milestones stretched me beyond my comfort zone, forcing me to confront self-doubt, challenge outdated beliefs, and step into opportunities that sometimes felt intimidating. Every credential I earned was proof of the internal growth that made my external achievements possible.

I've come to realize that growth isn't just about acquiring skills or professional accolades; it's about becoming more authentic. The more I grow, the more I understand who I am and what I value. I've learned how to express myself with clarity and kindness, to be transparent about my beliefs in a way that honors both my truth and the perspectives of others. I've refined my ability to contribute meaningfully without seeking to diminish anyone else. Most importantly, I've been able to strike a delicate but crucial balance: not shying away from my opinions or strengths while leading in a way that's rooted in compassion and respect, which is far more impactful.

Growth is not always glamorous. There are stretches of the process that feel messy and uncomfortable. There are setbacks that test your resolve and days when progress feels painfully slow. But that's the nature of growth—it's not a perfect linear path. And through it all, I've come to accept that stagnation equals death, while evolution equals life. The effort, though challenging, is what keeps us alive, passionately engaged, and aligned with our higher purpose.

The life you envision requires more than talent or ambition. It demands courage to confront limitations and discipline to work through them. Every step you take, no matter how small, is a declaration that you are capable of growing into the person you are meant to become. Every step is proof that you are committed to that life. Every step fuels your transformation.

You don't need permission or guarantees to start. Begin wherever you are, with whatever you have. Feed your mind with knowledge, surround yourself with people who challenge and inspire you, and stay connected to your vision.

The most beautiful part of this process is witnessing yourself changing from within. Each time you rise after failure, achieve a new milestone, and overcome a personal barrier, you rewire your brain and the way you think. You're embedding confidence into your psyche and neurology. You become better, not just for your own benefit, but so you can serve others from a more empowered and wise place.

CHAPTER 3: FOUNDATIONS OF A NETWORKING MINDSET

 ***Reader Reflection***: Reflect on a skill you've mastered and what it took to develop it. How can you apply your growth in that area to networking?

Every great structure begins with a strong foundation, one that is built to support the tests of time, and the storms and challenges that come with it. Your foundation, the lessons you've learned, the resilience you've forged, and the progress you've achieved, is no different. You have carefully constructed it through perseverance and determination, brick by brick, moment by moment. With this base, you are now ready to build higher, stronger, and more deliberately than before.

As we leave this chapter, take a moment to reflect on the groundwork you have laid. This is your unwavering support for the future you are creating. In the next chapter, you will learn the strategies and the tools you need to build on your foundation and create a thriving structure of success. With actionable insights and a clear direction, you will be prepared to adapt, grow, and seize opportunities—confidently and intentionally. I truly believe your best is yet to come, and the time to act is now.

Chapter 4: Strategic Networking

It's easy to look at networking as a daunting challenge, especially if you identify as an introvert. The idea of walking into a room full of strangers expecting to make meaningful connections can make you feel anxious, insecure, and full of self-doubt. But here's the truth: Networking isn't about being someone you're not. It's about discovering a process that works for you, a process that allows you to connect authentically, find your rhythm, and build a network rooted in trust and shared values.

When I go back to the beginning of my entrepreneurial journey, I'll be the first to admit I knew nothing about networking, though I unknowingly practiced it in small ways. I saw glimpses of it at church, in classes, during casual conversations with friends at the gym, and even out at nightclubs. However, when it came to strategic networking for business purposes, I was utterly green and, to be frank, terrified. I felt unsure, intimidated, insecure, and anxious. There were moments when depression gripped me, and the mere thought of showing up and connecting with others seemed impossible.

For a time, I was a wallflower. I tried to blend into the background, avoid eye contact, and stay parked on the sidelines. It was a painful experience, but one that introduced me to the significant yet hidden power of relationships. Every introduction, every reluctant handshake, every awkward first conversation slowly opened a new door. I began to understand how deeply relationships could impact me, the clients I served, and the work I wanted to amplify.

"Networking is not about being the loudest in the room; it's about leaving the most meaningful impact by showing genuine interest in others."

I grew into networking. The more I stepped out of my shell, the more doors opened. My approach shifted from survival to strategy, and my confidence grew as I began building a network of trusted colleagues and collaborators. From industry-specific networking events in the Palm Springs area to voluntary leadership roles on boards and nonprofits, I invested intentionally in connecting with others. At every step, I learned. Networking not only grew my business and credibility but helped me evolve into a leader comfortable in my own skin. The relationships I built changed everything, and I discovered something remarkably simple—networking is, at its core, about building meaningful relationships.

I want to help you do the same. The SAFER Networking framework is my way of capturing what I've learned and providing a roadmap for introverts who feel like networking just isn't for them. Rather than forcing yourself into extroverted molds, this framework allows you to approach networking on your own terms—strategically, authentically, and with purpose.

SAFER Networking

SAFER Networking helps you approach networking strategically while staying true to who you are. The acronym SAFER stands for:

1. **Select** - Choosing where, when, how and who to network with.

2. **Allow** - Giving yourself permission to have your own experience and connect in ways that work for you.

3. **Find** - Identifying and engaging partners or collaborators at events.

4. **Engage** - Breaking through superficial small talk to create real connections.

5. **Reflect & Reward** - Reviewing your efforts, reflecting on what worked, and celebrating even the smallest wins.

This framework draws from real-life scenarios and practical strategies. To make it more concrete, we'll walk through an ideal networking event as if we're planning it together.

1. Select

Imagine this scenario—you're at a perfect networking opportunity, tailored just for you. You get to choose the setting, the people, and the format. Now, ask yourself:

- **Where?** Would you feel more comfortable at a casual coffee meetup or a structured industry conference? Perhaps a local community event is the right start.

- **When?** Morning networking breakfasts can provide a very different energy compared to evening receptions. Pick a time when you're at your best.

- **Who?** Are you focusing on connecting with industry professionals, potential clients, or like-minded entrepreneurs? Be clear about the type of relationships you want to build.

- **How?** Would you feel more confident preparing questions ahead of time or role-playing scenarios with a trusted friend? Determine what strategies can ease your anxiety and set you up for success.

For me, this phase of the framework was pivotal. Early on, I underestimated the importance of being intentional about *where* and *how* I showed up. But as I began creating opportunities aligned with my *values* and *goals*, I noticed a shift. The room grew a little less intimidating, and the people around me were often those I wanted to know and connect with.

CHAPTER 4: STRATEGIC NETWORKING

 *Reader Reflection*: Plan a networking event you'd feel comfortable attending, from the location to the attendee list.

2. Allow

The second piece of SAFER Networking is about allowing yourself to take up space and engage authentically with those around you. This is a mindset shift. Remind yourself that you don't have to be the loudest in the room to be heard. Your presence, your perspective, and your story matter. Take a deep breath and give yourself permission to step outside your comfort zone. Breathe, and be present.

Beyond that, this phase is about engaging in ways that work for you. What one person does will not necessarily work for you, and vice versa. Learn from others by observing and using what feels authentic to you.

 Reader Reflection: Is there a mantra or a phrase to repeat to yourself if you find angst building up. Create your own way of reminding yourself you have value to add.

79

3. Find

When you get to the event, scan the venue for allies, like friends, colleagues, or individuals who radiate kindness. This just takes a few moments. Connect with these people first, and then branch out. Ask them to share their interests, goals, or values. I scan the room immediately at events to identify these people. Usually on my way to connect with them, I find others to connect with also.

You can't build trust overnight, so start small. Making a single meaningful connection is far more valuable than collecting dozens of business cards. You probably won't reach out to all of the people who gave you those cards anyway, so save some paper. Remember, just one new relationship is a win!

Reader Reflection: Recall the contacts you already know. Can you review the attendee list in advance to see who you know?. How can you create a habit to stop and scan the room upon arriving?

4. Engage

Ask questions that move the conversation beyond surface-level small talk. Start with openers like, "What inspired you to get into your business?" or "What's been the most exciting part of your work recently?" Thoughtful, open-ended questions create space for real connections. Ask questions that get people to talk about themselves. It takes the focus and pressure off of you to speak.

At my first event in Palm Springs, I decided to ask someone about the biggest lesson they learned in their career. Their response sparked a meaningful dialogue that led to a long-term connection. Genuine curiosity is magnetic. It forms a foundation of trust and reciprocity.

Reader Reflection: Brainstorm open-ended questions you could ask people about their family, business, leisure, or goals to create deeper connections.

5. Reflect & Reward

Finally, SAFER Networking concludes with reflection and celebration, steps often overlooked but essential to growth and evolution.

- **Review Your Efforts**

    After the event, take a moment to debrief with yourself. What went well? What could have been better? Identify ways to refine your approach for next time. The goal isn't to critique harshly but to learn.

- **Reflect on Your Wins**

    Even if you left the event without a stack of new contacts, consider the smaller victories. Did you initiate a conversation? How well did you listen? Did you challenge yourself to stay for an extra half hour? Those moments are worth celebrating. Reflect on what you learned about yourself in the experience.

- **Reward Yourself**

    Acknowledging your efforts doesn't have to mean extravagant gifts. Treat yourself to a relaxing evening, a favorite meal, or even a moment of quiet. By rewarding your effort, you reinforce positive behavior.

 Reader Reflection: After a real or imagined networking event, write a journal entry about what went well and how it felt.

Networking, especially as an introvert, is a skill that develops over time. It's not about pretending to be someone you're not or forcing uncomfortable interactions. It's about crafting a strategy that feels authentic and achievable, so you can empower yourself to build relationships with intention and integrity.

SAFER Networking is your guide to managing your individual energy to avoid burnout and make networking events more enjoyable and effective.

CHAPTER 4: STRATEGIC NETWORKING

By now, you've seen how intentional networking can transform from a daunting chore into a meaningful and fulfilling experience. It's not about how many people you meet; it's about the quality of those connections and the value you bring to each other. You can use the tools and perspectives you've explored in this chapter to build relationships based on trust, authenticity, and shared values.

Chapter 5 - Building and Sustaining Relationships

Strong relationships are the foundation of lasting success, in business and in life. They are the bridge between vision and reality, transforming ideas into opportunities propelled by trust, collaboration, and mutual investment. In a previous chapter, we laid the groundwork with principles and systems necessary for fostering connections. This chapter takes the concept further, empowering you with actionable strategies to transform fleeting interactions into meaningful, long-term relationships.

For me, making mistakes has been my greatest teacher in building and sustaining relationships. Early in my journey, I believed that with enough positive intention, strong relationships would just form naturally. But what happens when there isn't enough sustained effort? Missed opportunities, forgotten follow-ups, and the discomfort of letting a connection fade pushed me to approach relationships more intentionally. I remember reaching out to a promising business connection only to realize I'd lost momentum by not staying in touch consistently. Moments like these stung, but they also provided the spark for growth. Instead of shying away from my mistakes, I began to see them as valuable lessons—reminders that every relationship thrives on consistent attention, honest communication, and the courage to course-correct with humility when you need to most.

Building and sustaining authentic relationships in today's fast-paced world requires intentionality and effort. Beyond following up with a quick email or exchanging pleasantries at events, it's about creating a rhythm of consistent engagement that nurtures trust and adds value over time. With every new connection, you have the opportunity to enrich your network and uncover greater possibilities than either party could achieve alone. But how do you bridge the gap between making a connection and deepening it? How do you make sure no relationship falls through the cracks despite your busy schedule?

After missing an important follow-up one too many times, I started a simple, weekly check-in with my contacts. This routine reminded me to reconnect, offer support, or simply show genuine interest, and by doing so, I transformed my relationships from passive acquaintances to partners in business. Every stumble taught me a new way to be present and proactive. Over time, this reaction to my mistakes became the foundation of a consistent, authentic system for maintaining connections.

In this chapter, you'll learn a proven, repeatable system for follow-ups and relationship-building that fits seamlessly into your weekly routine. Whether it's sending a thoughtful note card, scheduling time for meaningful conversations, or celebrating milestones, you'll learn

CHAPTER 5 - BUILDING AND SUSTAINING RELATIONSHIPS

techniques to grow your influence while maintaining your authenticity. It's about leading with heart, putting people before profit, and ensuring every encounter is an opportunity to uplift others. Together, we'll explore ways to celebrate the people who make your business and life extraordinary.

Turning Small Talk Into Meaningful Connections

Whether you've met someone briefly at an event or had a professional introduction, the key to nurturing connections lies in how you follow up. Follow-ups should reflect real interest and thoughtfulness, and should not feel forced or transactional. In the past, I've done this mechanically just to "get it done," often at the expense of truly providing value and building genuine connection. This section focuses on crafting an effective follow-up plan, turning surface-level small talk into an ongoing dialogue that leads to trust and opportunity.

Take Linda, an enthusiastic but soft-spoken entrepreneur I met at a networking event years ago. Our chat began as small talk about her work in health coaching, but the conversation turned earnest when she shared her dream of building an online course. After the event, I sent Linda a personal note thanking her for the conversation and referencing the goals she shared. Along with the note, I provided a resource I thought might help her. It was a small gesture, but it opened the door to ongoing conversations. Over time, our connection grew into a mutually rewarding relationship of sharing insights and celebrating each other's wins.

This experience underscores how small, thoughtful actions can set the stage for long-lasting relationships. I always thought they had to be big, grand gestures. Not true! When you show that you're paying attention and honestly invested in someone else's success, it makes you memorable and builds trust.

The importance of thoughtfully following up became especially clear to me after instances when I failed to do it. Isn't that how it always works?! I realized that each missed opportunity could be a lost gateway to mutual support, learning, or collaboration. That insight changed my habits. I went from letting connections slip away to actively seeking ways to add value. Whether it's remembering a goal someone shared or sending a relevant article, consistent and intentional outreach builds stronger, trust-based connections.

"The foundation of strong relationships is trust, which we build through consistency. When we miss opportunities for follow-ups, they become chances for growth and renewed effort."

The First Step Is Organization

The first thing to do after meeting a new contact is get organized. Add their information to your database or any system you use, whether it's a CRM tool or a simple spreadsheet. Make sure you have their business details, mailing address, and also personal tidbits or the nature of your initial conversation. Over time, include birthdays, anniversaries, family information, common interests, and more. Details matter, and taking careful note of them demonstrates that you care.

A Heartfelt Touch

Next comes the step many overlook but it's also the step that makes all the difference: a personal note card. Sending a handwritten note is a timeless way to stand out and leave an impression. Reflect on something specific from your conversation or meeting, then write a thoughtful message that expresses appreciation about your encounter or admiration for their work.

I've learned that it's the personal touches, those extra steps that aren't seen as necessary, that truly create deeper connections. Early in my career, I was hesitant to send handwritten notes, worried they might seem old-fashioned or go unnoticed. But time and again, those personal notes have sparked conversation, gratitude, and collaboration. I've lost count how many times I've heard, "Your card is exactly what I needed today." What started as a simple remedy for past oversight became a trademark for the ways I love to connect.

 *Reader Reflection*: Take a moment to draft a follow-up note to someone you admire and recently met. Focus on what made your meeting memorable and include something personal to show authenticity.

Tools and Strategies to Deepen Relationships

Success in relationship-building is achieved by the small, consistent actions that create lasting bonds. When you develop a system for managing and nurturing your relationships, it gets easier to strengthen connections over time, regardless of how busy business and life gets. I carve time out of my day just for this purpose.

Below are some strategies I use, complete with actionable examples, to help you build and maintain meaningful connections:

- *Scheduled Follow-Ups*: Consistency is key when it comes to staying in touch. Dedicate time each week to go through your contact database and reconnect with people. Hint: Setting reminders or tasks makes this easier.

- *Quick Check-Ins*: Set aside 30 minutes on Monday mornings to send a thoughtful message to a few people. It could even be something as simple as, "Hey, I saw this article and thought of you. Hope you're well!"

CHAPTER 5 - BUILDING AND SUSTAINING RELATIONSHIPS

- *Personalized Meetings*: Perhaps each Friday, you schedule a coffee chat, lunch, or virtual call with someone in your network to catch up. Easy-peezy, and it's great to get out of the office.
- *Leverage Technology*: Tools like CRM software or even simple calendar reminders can help you stay on track. Apps like HubSpot or Google Calendar can notify you months after your last contact, ensuring you don't overlook any important connection.

I recall meeting Tom at a seminar years ago. During our brief conversation, he mentioned his company's upcoming 10th anniversary. I made a note and when the date came a few weeks later, I followed up with a congratulatory personal note. That simple gesture started a deeper connection that grew into a valuable mentorship. Today, I credit our relationship with helping me make some of my most important business decisions.

Follow-ups don't have to be grand. Simple gestures like sending a "thinking of you" text or scheduling a weekly coffee meeting help keep your connections alive. And with tech tools to streamline this process, you can ensure continuity without adding stress.

By creating a regular follow-up routine, you can be sure that even in times of chaos or growth, you're nurturing those critical relationships.

"See every connection as more than just professional. It's an opportunity to add value and celebrate what others bring to the table."

The Power of "Face-to-Face"

While digital tools make communication convenient, nothing replaces the depth of in-person interactions. Take time to arrange face-to-face moments that provide more opportunities for connection:

- *Casual Coffees and Lunches*: Reach out with a clear invitation, such as "I'd love to hear about your new projects over coffee. When are you free?" This approach lets people know you honestly value their time and story.

- *Shared Experiences*: Activities like attending a community event, visiting an art gallery, or joining a fitness class, a faith community, or interest groups together can create shared memories and build rapport.

- *Professional Events*: Attend conferences or meetups with the goal of intentionally catching up with current connections, while also meeting new ones.

These interactions nurture trust and understanding, which we can't always achieve through

CHAPTER 5 - BUILDING AND SUSTAINING RELATIONSHIPS

texts or emails. I've learned firsthand that small steps consistently applied over time produce amazing results. But don't take my word for it. Give it a go and see what results you create.

Handwritten Notes

Handwritten notes are a timeless way to leave a memorable impression. They show a level of thoughtfulness and effort that's rare in today's digital age. Here are specific ways to make the most impact using this method:

- *Thank-You Cards*: After meeting with someone or finishing a project, send a note expressing gratitude for their time, insight, or contribution. Get specific!

- *Congratulations Notes*: Whether they've hit a career milestone or shared great news with you, a quick note card recognizing the moment will mean a lot.

- *Holiday or Life Event Cards*: For holidays, birthdays, or major life changes, a simple message of acknowledgment makes people feel remembered and appreciated.

- **Helpful Tip**: Keep a box of notecards and stamps easily accessible, so it's always simple to take five minutes to write when inspiration strikes. Something short, sweet, and to the point is all you need. It doesn't have to be long. I'm lucky if I get four sentences on my note cards. Most importantly, have fun with it!

It's amazing how a small, personal gesture can undo the impact of earlier neglect. I keep these tools close as reminders of the lessons that experience, and yes, my mistakes, can teach. If you're ever unsure where to begin, start small and start personal. Your network will feel the difference.

Reader Reflection: Create a checklist for staying in touch with people in an authentic and meaningful way. Consider ways to be consistent without overwhelming yourself.

Celebrating Your Connections

Relationships thrive when they are nurtured, celebrated, and valued. Taking time to recognize the people who have supported you, referred you for opportunities, or stood by you over the years can deepen bonds and create a ripple of positivity. Here are actionable ways to celebrate your connections:

- *Highlight Their Contributions*: Elevating others in your network strengthens relationships and shines a light on each person's strengths. Do this publicly when possible for maximum impact!

- *Social Media Shout-Outs*: Post about a colleague's recent achievement, tagging them in your message and sharing why it's worth celebrating. Even better, pick up the phone and call them

CHAPTER 5 - BUILDING AND SUSTAINING RELATIONSHIPS

about the post. You'll stand out more than likes or comments!

- **Client or Partner Features**: Dedicate a section in your blog or newsletter to showcase the incredible work someone in your network is doing. Every month, I highlight three local businesses in my newsletters. It's fun, costs me nothing, and takes a small amount of time to highlight them.

- **Celebratory Events**: Plan occasional gatherings, whether virtual or in person, to bring your network together and publicly recognize milestones, wins, or contributions. This can be done with little to no financial investment. You could do a movie night, meet at a restaurant, or go all out and throw an appreciation party.

These efforts make people feel appreciated while reinforcing your role as a connector within your community.

 "Dedicate time for weekly follow-ups. Send thoughtful messages, schedule conversations, or recognize someone's achievements to deepen connections."

Express Gratitude Publicly and Privately

Gratitude leaves a lasting and memorable impression. When you express gratitude, you extend kindness, and you create an inviting culture for others to do the same. Here are some ideas to show genuine appreciation:

- **Private Acts of Gratitude**: Write a heartfelt thank-you card to a contact and include a personal story about how their help impacted you. Send a small, tailored gift when appropriate, such as a book you know they'll enjoy or a gift card to their favorite coffee shop.

- **Public Displays of Gratitude**: Use formats like LinkedIn to write an appreciation post, tagging a mentor or collaborator and sharing their positive impact on your growth or success. Do this on top of making the phone call I mentioned previously and you'll knock it out of the park.

- **Special Touches**: On anniversaries of key experiences (like someone's hire date if they work with you or the day of a successful project launch), reach out with a note or call to acknowledge the moment for them. Share specifically what you appreciate about working with them.

Small yet thoughtful gestures build goodwill and an ongoing cycle of trust and connection. Keep it light when appropriate, and have fun connecting with your sphere and building meaningful relationships.

CHAPTER 5 - BUILDING AND SUSTAINING RELATIONSHIPS

 *Reader Reflection*: Write a gratitude list of five people you value most in your network. Then, turn this act of reflection into action by writing each of them a note card and sharing your appreciation.

Building and sustaining relationships is an ongoing process that thrives on consistency, authenticity, and engagement. In this chapter, you learned a structured and intentional approach for transforming new contacts into trusted allies. By following the plan for follow-ups, integrating tools and routines for staying connected, and celebrating the people who enhance your life and business, you have a system in place that maximizes the potential of every relationship.

And if you miss a connection or stumble at any point, remember: The most powerful moments of growth often come not from our wins, but from what we learn from our mistakes. Every missed call, every delayed "thank you" has within it an opportunity for growth and understanding. With every adjustment and every re-do, you strengthen your ability to build a community rooted in trust and growth.

For relationships to truly thrive, they require consistent engagement and connection. This is where storytelling comes into play. Storytelling is one of the most profound ways to breathe life into your conversations. While systems and strategies provide the structure to build connections, stories create the bridge that deepens them. A well-told story can transcend surface-level interactions, helping you communicate your values, share lessons, and evoke emotions. It can transform acquaintances into advocates driven by a shared sense of understanding and purpose.

When you share authentic stories of challenges you've faced, victories you've celebrated, or poignant lessons you've learned, you invite others to find common ground. These narratives, your authentic stories, make you relatable, foster empathy, and allow your unique voice to shine. More importantly, they offer others an opportunity to see how their own experiences align with yours, bridging gaps and reinforcing trust.

This next chapter will guide you in crafting and sharing meaningful stories that resonate with your audience and strengthen your bonds, ensuring you sustain your connections and enrich them at their core. Together, we'll uncover how to harness the power of your personal narrative to inspire, engage, and continue growing alongside the people who matter most in your professional and personal journey.

Chapter 6: The Art of Storytelling

"A well-told story can transcend surface-level interactions, helping you share your values and lessons, and evoke emotions that strengthen connections."

Storytelling is an unsung hero behind many meaningful connections we make, both in business and in life. As professionals, introverts, and, most importantly, as individuals pursuing growth, stories give depth and clarity to our values. They allow us to share who we are and what we care about, all while creating space for others to do the same. For those of us who may not thrive in the spotlight, stories deliver structure, purpose, and connection—without sacrificing authenticity.

Over the years, I've learned that storytelling doesn't require grand, dramatic tales. In fact, the most memorable moments in my network did not begin on big stages but in simple everyday gestures. I began to understand the value of storytelling when I started producing video content for my real estate business. Early on, these videos weren't polished productions; they were heartfelt stories about helping clients, overcoming obstacles in a hectic market, or simply the joy of closing. It was in those moments—sharing the story of a couple buying their first home or documenting the challenges of selling a home during the summer—that I saw engagement, and trust, flourish. The feedback I received from viewers was not about facts, figures, or credentials. Instead, people remembered the feeling, the transformation, and the shared humanity within each story. As I've often said, facts tell, but stories sell. Well, I didn't come up with that quote, but I still LOVE it and use it!

That ability to connect found its way into my elevator pitches and networking conversations. Rather than rattling off accolades, titles and market stats, I led with a brief story—snippets about helping a client overcome doubt and land their dream home, or the mistakes I've made and the lessons I now use to guide clients. These stories turn introductions into memorable engagements, giving listeners a reason to continue the conversation.

Throughout this book, you've seen these types of anecdotes woven into everything, from follow-up strategies in Chapter 3 to stories about celebrating others in Chapter 4 and creating lasting impressions in Chapter 5. Each chapter has built toward this one, illustrating how real-life narratives can open doors, build trust, and boost personal and business success.

CHAPTER 6: THE ART OF STORYTELLING

 *"Sharing stories of past mistakes and the lessons you've learned makes you relatable and highlights your authenticity."*

As we dive in, it's important to know: The art of storytelling is a skill, honed through practice, reflection, and, yes, mistakes. My own storytelling skills came from sharing successes, but even more so, from openly discussing mistakes and how they altered and shaped my approach to connections. One moment that stands out is when a missed follow-up almost cost me a valuable transaction. Admitting that oversight, and then working to rebuild trust, became one of my core stories, highlighting the importance of honesty, consistency, and vulnerability in my interactions.

When you frame your actions, no matter how small, into a story, you move beyond transactions to transformation. You become memorable, not just for what you do, but for how you make others feel and grow.

Part I: Identifying Your Core Stories

Every leader, connector, and introvert has moments that shape who we are—pivotal experiences, challenges, and victories that define our growth and mindset. These become our core stories, our most valuable storytelling assets. These stories are the foundation of your narrative and your brand.

Some of the richest stories arise not only from big moments that change our life trajectory, but also from small moments we can easily overlook. Each of these moments, no matter how small, has the potential to forge a connection, teach a lesson, and make someone feel that you see and value them.

Let's expand on how to find and craft them for yourself, using examples from my own path:

1. **Reflect on Turning Points**

Start with moments that changed you. For me, a major turning point came from an open house that didn't go as planned. I had prepared every detail—awesome staging, lighting, and snacks. But turnout was disappointing, and I felt like I'd missed the mark. Instead of retreating, I took time to reflect on what went wrong and what I could control. Later, I shared that honesty in a video, owning the lesson and how I adjusted my outreach. That story became an anchor point—a tale of learning from setbacks and connecting with my audience's own experiences of falling short and bouncing back. Your own turning points may be career pivots, bold follow-ups, or even missed opportunities that inspired fresh resolve.

2. **Explore Lessons You've Learned**

Every experience carries a lesson. I'll never forget the time I sent a video message to a client celebrating her new job. I referenced advice I'd given her during our first meeting (a story I shared back in Chapter 2), drawing a clean line between past support and present achievement. She responded with more than thanks—she referred me to three connections who have become chapters in my own storybook of connections. Think about the lessons you've passed along, big or small, and how they echo in your community.

3. Identify Emotional Highs and Lows

Storytelling is about emotional resonance and connection. I still remember when I handed over keys to a single father closing on his first home, he felt so much pride it was contagious. Or the quiet anxiety I felt creeping in before pressing "record" on my first real estate testimonial video. Sharing these highs and lows, like the time I nervously attended my first business peer accountability group, lets your network know you're not invincible. Your journey, with all its ups and downs, mirrors theirs, creating a powerful bridge of empathy.

"Practice storytelling with your introductions by sharing a story instead of sharing credentials. It will leave a memorable impression."

---

4. Write Your Stories Down

Don't rely on memory alone. It probably won't work. I've made it a habit to journal after key meetings, reflecting on what worked, what didn't, and what surprised me. For example, a simple check-in text—"Saw this article and thought of you"—sparked an unexpected partnership later on. Writing these moments down helps you see the emerging themes in your story, like generosity, resilience, and consistent follow-through. It also gives you a resource to draw from when you want to share stories in casual conversation or formal introductions.

5. Focus on Universal Takeaways

What can others learn from your journey? When I recount how sending a handwritten note led to a new referral partner or how openly admitting a mistake built more trust than perfection ever could, it's not just my own lesson. It's a blueprint others can relate to and apply. Make your stories useful—offer them as a roadmap, cautionary tale, or a spark of encouragement for the next person.

6. Refine and Practice

Storytelling is a skill that strengthens with daily practice. I practice by sharing stories in low-pressure settings, over a casual coffee or even reflecting with family. Over time, I've noticed my stories becoming tighter and more resonant; sometimes I tell them in two minutes, sometimes in 10. Resharing the story of a negotiation I navigated well, or an unexpected act of kindness not only clarifies my message for others but deepens my own sense of purpose. The more you tell your stories, the clearer and more natural your voice will become.

These strategies empower you to embrace your natural talents, like observation, empathy, and intentionality, without performance pressure. A thoughtful, well-told story can leave a greater impression than the loudest voice in the room.

CHAPTER 6: THE ART OF STORYTELLING

Reader Reflection: Think of a small action from your professional or personal life—a follow-up, a thank you, a helpful introduction—that sparked momentum or changed the path of a relationship. What did you learn, and what might your story teach someone else?

Part II: Crafting Magnetic Introductions

The first moments of any connection are precious, and brief. You have only a few seconds to captivate, reassure, and inspire people to remember you. Storytelling, rather than reciting credentials, brings color and warmth. It brings heart into it.

In Chapter 3, we discussed the power of micro-moments: small, specific stories in introductions. These are particularly effective in networking events and elevator pitches. Instead of saying, "I help people with real estate transactions," I'll share, "I help families get the keys to a home they never thought they'd own." Or, referencing my practice of celebrating others, I might open with, "I invest in people's success, one handwritten note and phone call at a time."

When I began including stories in my elevator pitches, I noticed people leaning in—both figuratively and literally. At a recent lunch, instead of giving a boring introduction, I shared how an acknowledging LinkedIn

105

post sparked a connection. Heads nodded, conversation followed, and the conversation led to more connections.

Experiment with your own story-based introductions:

- Recall a time you went beyond expectations—maybe organizing a service provider connection for a client or helping a colleague navigate a challenge.
- Relate that moment to your mission, showing how it informs the value you bring.
- Most importantly, infuse your introduction with care for the person you are talking to and their journey, making it about connection as much as accomplishment.

Reader Reflection: For your next introduction, consider highlighting a moment of genuine support rather than a list of titles. How might this change the dynamic, and how could it influence your new relationship?

Part III: Storytelling in Sales and Everyday Networking

Many view sales and networking as a series of pitches, but the reality is far more. Authentic stories engage, educate, and inspire action—not just because they entertain, but

CHAPTER 6: THE ART OF STORYTELLING

because they illustrate outcomes, highlight values, and foster community.

For me, many of these stories are about small ways I connect with others: in a Monday morning message of encouragement, a call-out of someone's win in a group, or a surprise "thank you" card in a world that has grown increasingly digital, transactional, and numb. These are routines and rituals (see Chapter 2) that tell my story of reliability, generosity, and attention. When I mail a handwritten note after a closing, I'm not just closing business; I'm opening a new chapter with that person, inviting them back, and showing that my support extends beyond the transaction.

One of my favorite habits is publicly celebrating others, both on social media (as seen in Chapter 5) and in private messages. Recently, after recognizing a client's milestone on LinkedIn and following up with a call, not only did our connection deepen, but they shared my story within their network, leading to new connections. This cycle of celebrating others, following up, and sharing the story of how it all came together consistently builds credibility.

Reader Reflection: Think back to an instance when you did something small that added to your reputation, like celebrating someone's accomplishment or someone celebrating yours. How did that recognition impact your relationship? How can you tell this story in your next sales pitch?

Storytelling transforms the ordinary into the extraordinary. Every email, handshake, and message can be the start of a new narrative for you and those you serve. Start small—share a lesson you learned or a moment when someone showed you kindness. Bring these stories into your routine and let them foster momentum, trust, and opportunity.

As you master the art of storytelling, you'll realize the power lies not just in captivating others, but in empowering and inspiring them to write new stories with you. Your journey, filled with challenges, lessons, and victories, is the guide others may need. As you continue to share, reflect, and connect, the impact of your story—and the stories of those around you—will multiply, building a network rooted in authenticity, growth, and success.

The next chapter focuses on platforms for storytelling: social media and video. Social media isn't just about connecting with people and talking about life's ups and downs. For me, social media and video are ways to provide and demonstrate value. I LOVE creating content that is engaging and informative. If we think of everything we post on social media as mini stories, we will attract bigger audiences and make connections with people who resonate with our journey.

Chapter 7 - Social Media & Video

In our world today, we now have access to game-changing tools to improve the way we communicate, connect, and create. Social media and video offer unparalleled platforms to amplify messages and engage with others. These tools hold the power to transform your reach, shape your brand, and unlock opportunities you may not have thought possible. It's time to step into the role of a creator and harness these powerful mediums to their full potential.

To demonstrate just how much these platforms can nurture connection, let me share a story from my early days on LinkedIn. I commented thoughtfully on a post from a leader in my industry—sharing an insight rather than simply agreeing with their post. To my surprise, not only did the person reply and connect, but their response sparked a flurry of messages from others in the thread, leading to several other connections. That one moment of value-focused engagement became a catalyst for multiple long-term connections *off* the platform (aka in real life). The lesson? When you show up authentically and contribute value, you can create as many opportunities online as you do face to face.

 *"Social media isn't about perfection; it's about authenticity. Authenticity always outshines a manicured façade."*

Picture your dream client scrolling through their social feed. Among the clutter of content, they pause on your video or post. Something about it resonates with them—it's clear, authentic, and speaks directly to their challenges or goals. They click. They comment. They share. They may even make the decision to take action by following your work, visiting your website, or enrolling in your services. You have brought them into your community. That moment, that connection, is the spark that fuels momentum. It certainly was for me.

I've witnessed how simple, personal outreach through social media can plant seeds for deeper connections. A client of mine once reached out to thank someone for sharing a helpful article in a Facebook group. That thank-you message didn't just stop at gratitude; it led to a conversation, a Zoom call, and eventually, a project that brought value to both of our networks. This is the magic of connections through social media: When you lead with appreciation and a spirit of giving value, you open doors that can lead anywhere.

The truth is, I wasn't always confident in my ability to succeed with social media or video. I remember how foreign it felt to plan, create, and put myself out there, especially in a format that can feel soooo vulnerable. Honestly, I hated it! But I also knew how transformational

CHAPTER 7 - SOCIAL MEDIA & VIDEO

it could be. With mindful strategies, practice, and an eagerness to learn, I grew into the role of an effective content creator. Today, I use social media and video to expand my reach, share my authentic self, and make connections that inspire trust. Stories like these, from my journey and those I've witnessed, illustrate a simple truth—anyone can achieve success with the right tools and mindset.

This chapter gives you a step-by-step guide to leverage social media and video in ways that align with you. *It's not about becoming someone else*—it's about amplifying who you already are. Whether you're nervous about being on camera or still finding the confidence to share your ideas, this chapter will meet you where you are and help you grow. We'll discuss how to select the platforms that speak directly to your audience, how to craft and share meaningful content, and how to measure results so that every step moves you closer to your goals. Above all, this chapter will equip you with a mindset of creativity and action. You are not here to fit into someone else's mold—you are here to reshape your business as you create connections that matter most.

Get ready to step boldly into your potential. There's no better time to make your mark.

Understanding the Platforms

Social media is vast and dynamic, and each platform serves different objectives and different audiences. Think of social media platforms as tools in a well-equipped toolbox—each has a function capable of shaping your message in different ways. For example, LinkedIn is a haven for professionals looking to establish authority, share thought leadership, and network with others in their industries. Instagram, rooted in visual storytelling, is perfect for showcasing photos, videos, and moments of creativity. TikTok, with its lighthearted and educational short-form videos, delivers bursts of inspiration capable of reaching wide, diverse audiences quickly. For long-form content, YouTube is the king, offering space for detailed content and tutorials with complete immersion into each topic.

Choosing the right platforms requires an understanding of your audience. Where do they spend their time? What are their challenges and interests? What kind of media grabs their attention? This will require a bit of Google or AI research if you don't already know.

Instead of spreading yourself thin across every available platform, prioritize quality over quantity. Focus on the platforms where your voice resonates the most. By narrowing your efforts, you can develop content that is not only impactful but also authentic to your brand. I have learned that creating long-form content for YouTube is my superpower. Then, I repurpose that long-form into blogs, shorts and graphic posts for other social platforms.

Let me share another story that illustrates how the right platform can unlock new opportunities. Linda, an entrepreneur who attended one of my courses, used Instagram to share snapshots of her health coaching journey. Her posts were authentic, focusing on small wins and struggles. One day, she received a comment from someone in her target audience (someone who later

CHAPTER 7 - SOCIAL MEDIA & VIDEO

became a long-term client) because of the authenticity of her stories and how much they resonated. This experience turned a public social post into a high-value connection, simply because she used storytelling on the right platform.

Reader Reflection: Picture your ideal client scrolling through social media. What kind of post immediately grabs their attention? Is it a short, impactful video? A text post with a powerful message? Start crafting content ideas tailored to their interests and preferences.

Crafting a Compelling Video Strategy

Video content is one of the most effective ways to engage audiences. It can bring your personality and expertise to life, allow your audience to connect with you beyond words or visuals, and create an emotional bond that builds trust. Whether it's a raw, spontaneous live stream, a short, or a masterpiece you carefully produced and edited, video content is your opportunity to invite others into your world and story.

Tom, a past client, struggled to see the value of video until we experimented with simple check-in clips. In his first video, he mentioned his company's upcoming anniversary and offered a candid reflection on the journey up to that point. The response was encouraging—clients old and new reached out to congratulate him, and one even referred him to a new client. Tom was amazed to see how being open and vulnerable in video could spark engagement and even impact results.

"Experiment with different formats and platforms to find what resonates with your target audience."

Before hitting the record button, it's important to start with a purpose. What do you want your audience to take away from the video? Is it inspiration, a solution to a problem, or simply a spark of joy? When you focus on providing value, the creation process becomes more empowering and rewarding. Storytelling also plays an important role. A compelling narrative captures attention and elicits emotional responses, increasing the likelihood of deeper connection.

For those who feel intimidated by the idea of being on camera, take heart. Start where you are. Focus on your message, and remember that growth comes through persistence and practice. You don't need to be perfect; you just need to be willing to start. We'll go into this deeper in Chapter 10.

CHAPTER 7 - SOCIAL MEDIA & VIDEO

Reader Reflection: Picture your ideal client watching one of your videos. What lingers in their mind? Does it make them feel seen, heard, and inspired? Draft a script and video post around that feeling.

Building Engagement

Once my content is live, engagement is where the magic happens—it shapes the conversation and builds momentum. Authentic, consistent interaction is key to earning trust and creating connections that last. By repurposing a single video into Instagram reels, TikTok clips, and blog posts, I'm able to leverage content in multiple formats and expand my reach while delivering a consistent message.

I learned the value of thoughtful engagement through another relationship I built over social media. After making a thank-you post acknowledging the help of someone in my network, that public kudos led to a flurry of direct messages. I found myself reconnecting with old connections, scheduling calls, and discovering opportunities—all because of one post. This is the power of engagement; it's not just numbers, but real, authentic connection.

Responding to comments, reacting to messages, and genuinely initiating conversations with your audience creates a culture where everyone feels seen and heard.

When people know their voice matters to you, they're more likely to stick around and even become advocates for your brand. Also, the more you engage, the more the algorithm works for your benefit.

Reader Reflection: Think back to a post or video that resonated with your audience. Was it the tone, the timing, or the topic? Reflect on how you can replicate that success in a new way.

Measuring Impact

Analytics may seem daunting, but when you understand them correctly, they can provide a treasure trove of insights. Data-driven strategies help you refine your content, ensuring that each post and video is more impactful than the last. Speaking from experience, I've been able to evolve into a more effective creator because I've put time and resources into understanding my metrics. If you want to see meaningful growth, trust me—the fastest way is to start tracking your results, analyzing what they are telling you, and then adjusting as needed.

"Set a manageable content schedule and focus on consistency over quantity to build momentum."

CHAPTER 7 - SOCIAL MEDIA & VIDEO

A friend once told me that studying the performance of his LinkedIn posts changed his approach to content. He noticed a spike in engagement with storytelling-focused updates—especially when he celebrated others' achievements. Inspired, he made it a routine to highlight his colleagues' wins and share honest kudos for their work. That small shift tripled his engagement rates within months. Through reflection and data, he learned that celebrating others not only brings value to his community but also expands his digital influence.

By adopting a data-driven mindset, I have grown as a content creator and as a communicator with a purpose. Tracking results isn't just about numbers; for me, it's about uncovering patterns, learning from the process, and continuously evolving to deliver value-based, authentic messages.

 Reader Reflection: Reflect on a moment when a new insight from your data improved your strategy. What lesson did you take away, and how did it influence your approach moving forward?

Social media and video provide incredible opportunities to amplify your message and make an impact in today's fast-paced world. We just illuminated the importance of selecting the right platforms, crafting content that resonates and connects emotionally, and building engagement with your audience. The stories we've shared—from Linda's Instagram connection to Tom's courageous first video and the ripple effect of authentic engagement—make it clear that lasting professional connections can begin with small, sincere interactions.

Remember, these platforms are not about perfection—they're about connection. With patience, creativity, and determination, anyone can harness these tools to share their unique value with the world. Now, it's time to take what you've learned and put it into action. The next section will help you integrate these strategies into your vision, ensuring you create impactful content and measurable outcomes. Embrace the practice—don't wait to be perfect. Every effort, even one that starts small, counts toward your evolution.

Now that we've laid the foundation in the first section, "The Work," you're ready to put it into practice, or "Into Action," in the second section. Putting it into action isn't about doing it perfectly. Learning is about making mistakes and adjusting along the way. No one hits a bullseye the first time they shoot an arrow at a target. Think of this next section as practice, not about an ideal you must achieve before you put yourself out there.

Ok. Let's get moving!

Section II - Into Action

So far, we've unpacked what it truly means to build meaningful relationships, from establishing genuine connections based on authenticity and empathy, to cultivating trust through consistent actions and authentic connections. We've delved into the importance of setting healthy boundaries to protect your energy and well-being, navigating challenging conversations with empathy and confidence, and growing a powerful, supportive network, even as an introvert. You've explored practical frameworks, actionable mindset shifts, and proven strategies all carefully designed to equip you for personal and professional success. Together, we've examined how small, intentional actions can lead to lasting connections, and how mastering the skill of relationship-building can open doors to opportunities you might never have imagined.

As we transition to the next phase of your journey, we come to the most critical step: putting these insights into practice. No matter how much you prepare, how many strategies you learn, or how many tools you gather, real growth only happens through action—when you step into new situations, take risks, and learn through experience. This is where theory meets reality, and often, it's not an easy step.

To illustrate, let's go back to my experience with Tom. Remember I followed up with Tom after a seminar and he mentioned his company's 10-year anniversary. As you'll recall, I made a note of this and reached out on the anniversary date with a congratulatory message. Tom admitted the gesture touched him; it was a small but thoughtful reminder that I had listened and cared. That action marked a turning point, deepening our connection which ultimately developed into a mentorship. It's a powerful example of how acting on what you learn about others, no matter how minor it seems, can transform an acquaintance into an ally.

Growth requires courage, the courage to initiate and to face uncertainty, but also the courage to embrace failure and to keep going when things don't go as planned. It is in these moments of discomfort that we learn the deepest lessons. While success can be a powerful motivator, it is often our mistakes that have the most impact. Every misstep gives us valuable feedback, a chance to reassess, pivot, and adapt, strengthening our resilience and ability to thrive in relationships.

One of the most important things you can do for your growth is develop the mindset to see failure as an essential part of the process rather than something you need to avoid. You can redefine those moments of falling short as turning points, opportunities to refine your approach and become stronger. Mistakes reveal gaps you might not have noticed. They teach you persistence, patience, and humility while adding to your toolbox of knowledge. Through failure, you gain the wisdom and confidence to handle future challenges with greater ease.

I've seen this firsthand: reaching out to someone and not getting a response or leaving a meeting that fell

SECTION II - INTO ACTION

flat. It feels discouraging at first, but with every setback, there is something to learn. Maybe it's how to refine communication, follow up differently, or simply recognize that timing plays a role. Over time, these experiences build our adaptability and emotional intelligence.

This next section invites you to take everything you've learned so far and apply it to real-world settings. This might mean starting a conversation with someone new, addressing a long-standing conflict, or stepping into unfamiliar situations where growth feels both exciting and intimidating. Engage in environments that challenge your perspective, require vulnerability, or demand more effort than you anticipated. But remember, growth isn't about doing everything perfectly. It's about showing up, staying curious, and having the courage to learn from every outcome—especially the unexpected ones.

True growth lies in your willingness to celebrate small wins and approach every interaction, whether it ends in success or setback, as an opportunity to evolve. Each step forward brings you closer to the meaningful, authentic relationships you want to build. Like Linda, Tom, and countless others who have taken that first step out of their comfort zones, you will have a profound impact on yourself and others through your actions, no matter how small. So take that first step and embrace your journey! The world is full of opportunities to connect, grow, and thrive, if you're willing to take the leap.

Let's jump into action!

Chapter 8: Mindset Matters Most

The mindset you carry is your foundation for change; it's a bridge between your current self and your goals. When I talk about a mindset makeover, I'm not speaking about radical overnight transformation or chasing some unattainable idea of perfection. It's about steady, consistent progress, choosing small intentional actions every day and aligning who you are with who you're becoming. My journey and the stories I share here show that real-life trials, setbacks, and moments of insight build lasting transformation.

I learned this first-hand when the "dot.bomb" crisis forced me out of my dream job as an introvert in IT. Suddenly, my whole sense of identity evaporated. That crisis thrust me into entrepreneurship not by choice, but by necessity. I needed to pay the bills. So I struggled, feeling small, insecure, anxious, and uncertain. But even in those early years, I discovered that my introverted nature wasn't a liability, it was a strength. This chapter draws on the tools and techniques that I learned or created that kept me moving forward, and the stories that unfolded from this mindset shift.

In today's relentlessly connected world, prioritizing your mindset can seem counterintuitive. We're constantly told to move faster, chase more, do everything now. Yet, again and again, I've seen and experienced how pausing to create quiet space leads to clarity and connection. When my real estate business flatlined in the mid-2000s because my partner and I had stopped marketing and networking, it became painfully clear: Action matters, but intentional reflection matters even more. Later, in another valley of my career, I looked over at my expired real estate license after being fired as a counselor. Giving myself space to feel, reflect, and reconnect with what I valued, I found the clarity to re-enter real estate with renewed energy.

For clients like Jason, that clarity came through digital detoxes and journaling at the start of each week—simple rituals that opened him up to unexpected inner resources. For Karen, it was a daily 15-minute walk before meetings, a practice I've also used, which grounded her and led to deep conversations. By embracing grounding habits like meditation, monthly sessions dedicated to vision-setting, journaling, and reflection, you can foster resilience, focus, and perspective that you need to thrive as a business owner, leader, or connector.

As you read this chapter, I challenge you: Pause and breathe. Picture yourself at those crossroads, maybe unexpected layoffs, overwhelming setbacks, big wins you've worked years for. Ask yourself: Are your daily actions and activities moving you closer to your vision? Let the examples, practices, and reflection prompts in these pages serve as both a mirror and a roadmap for your next bold steps.

CHAPTER 8: MINDSET MATTERS MOST

The Power of Mindset in Relationship-Building

This chapter is about becoming someone who naturally attracts the connections, opportunities, and experiences you seek. Empowerment, confidence, and a resilient mindset aren't given or gifts; you earn them through repeated, intentional alignment of your actions with your values.

I learned this as a new entrepreneur: After studying for my real estate broker's exam, I faced two painful failed attempts in a row on the state exam. My ego and confidence took a beating, but each setback forced me to ask for help, try new prep strategies, and embrace humility as a strength. By the third attempt, with the right mindset and strategy, I finally passed the exam, and the lessons I learned forged connections with colleagues and clients. This experience taught me that growth is rarely linear; it takes persistent action, adaptability, and reflection to build growth.

"Quiet moments for reflection often lead to the greatest clarity. They allow you to break patterns and align with the goals that fuel progress."

Let's talk about Diane. She's a quiet consultant who transformed her networking by sending gratitude notes and customized resources to people she wanted to connect with. Her story mirrors my own journey from viewing introversion as a liability to leveraging it as an asset. Or take Linda and her courageous follow-up message to a new connection, which launched into a partnership and leadership opportunities. For me, founding my first BNI chapter was a crash course in relationship-building: I moved from shy newcomer to connector, value-add partner, and ultimately someone people sought out for collaboration.

The shift from chasing external validation to embodying confidence changed everything. By fully embracing frameworks like SIDE and RADICAL Focus, discussed in Chapter 3, my network expanded and the trust and connections in my circles deepened. By being consistently authentic and living your values, you will attract the *right* people. When you become known for follow-through, encouragement, and being present, doors open easily and sometimes, in the most unexpected and rewarding ways.

Stillness and Reflection

Stillness isn't the absence of action; it's the ground from which powerful, creative action emerges. It's where you find insights buried under routines. For introverts and thoughtful leaders alike, stillness is a strategic asset.

After my company laid me off from my beloved IT job, I was reeling and lost. Instead of immediately grasping for the next thing, I spent weeks in reflection questioning, journaling, and meditating. That deliberate pause gave birth to my focus on growth, long before I understood its impact. Later, as I faced rejections trying

CHAPTER 8: MINDSET MATTERS MOST

to pass my real estate broker's license exam, I set aside time for prep weekends and reflection, cultivating the steady resolve that finally helped me succeed on my third try.

Sunday evening reviews, which I started after a business coaching mentor suggested it, have become one of my most cherished rituals. During this time, I look over my week, reflecting on how I showed up for others, who might need a lift, or what unfinished conversations need follow-up. Once, I reached out to a colleague who seemed withdrawn, simply to check in. That call rekindled our connection and resulted in a referral relationship that neither of us had seen coming.

Another practice I do is pausing for a few intentional breaths before every client call, which helps me show up to conversations grounded and authentic. This leads to deeper rapport in conversations. During a particularly difficult stretch in my business, when I gave myself a strict "empowerment hour" each morning—half reflection, half outreach—this sparked new connections, and also gave me fresh ideas for the Bowtie Coach brand.

You can use stillness to create the space needed to break out of reaction mode and move intentionally toward your goals. Whether it's a morning meditation, a mind-clearing walk, or a "vision session" mapping your next steps, these habits invite greater clarity, and with clarity comes better, more authentic connections.

Reader Reflection: Choose a stillness practice that's right for you. Maybe it's meditating for five minutes before your workday, journaling about a lesson you've learned after a networking event or call, or blocking Sunday evening to review your week. Consider reading *One Small Step Can Change Your Life* by Dr. Robert Maurer like I did a few years ago, and discover how incremental change, rooted in stillness, shapes transformation.

Inputs and Focus

What you consume mentally, whether it's news, emails, conversations, even the energy of a room, it all can shape your focus, emotions, and ultimately your path. I learned this when an early-career obsession with always staying informed left me scattered, disorganized, annoyed, and exhausted. It wasn't until I did a full information and digital audit—unsubscribing, unfollowing, trimming my digital interactions—that I experienced a new level of clarity and productivity. Wowza!

This new focus paid dividends. I joined a mastermind book club dedicated to learning. There, my growth flourished with theory, practical actions, connections, and mutual goals. This also led directly to a connection with Alex, now a member of my network who helped me land a consulting gig with an innovative

CHAPTER 8: MINDSET MATTERS MOST

founder. Every high-quality input I spent my time on—personal conversations, books, podcasts—formed a bridge to beneficial connections.

Focusing my daily actions has been a recurring lifeline. During periods of overwhelm in my entrepreneurial journey, I practiced 30-minute sprints of uninterrupted work before networking events or follow up calls. When I hung my real estate license after a career reset, I dedicated my sharpest hours to important follow-ups. This practice led me to double my average for transactions in that first year back as a realtor.

But focus isn't only about productive action. I've found that it's also about reclaiming your joy and curiosity. A pivotal moment came when I realized I was more energized after a walk with a peer or a mid-day reading break than after hours hunched over a screen. High-quality connections and creative problem-solving are always strongest when my mind is properly "fed"—with positive inputs and intentional downtime.

 Reader Reflection: Select and timeblock two focus hours each day, protecting them from all distraction—emails, apps, social media. Notice how your energy shifts. Write about your experience and results in your journal during your weekly review and reflection.

Breaking Patterns and Embracing Growth

Change starts by breaking patterns that keep us small. My biggest growth leaps came after I confronted my own resistance: negative self-talk, fear of failure, or habits that weren't serving me. After the dot.bomb layoff, my instinct was to bury myself in regret, but those feelings only kept me stuck. It wasn't until I started asking for help, first in test prep, later in business, that new opportunities appeared.

A lesson that sticks with me is from when I built my first BNI chapter. At first, I dreaded asking for help and hosting events. But in the process of building (and rebuilding) strategic connections through BNI, I was forced to break my habit of under-communicating and my reluctance to follow up. Each new conversation, each invitation, was a step out of my comfort zone. The ripple effect: We went from needing referrals and connections for new members to building a thriving community for everyone—and it was one where people valued me.

 "Start a mindset practice by reflecting daily—meditate, journal, or identify one limiting belief to challenge and replace with a growth-oriented thought."

Linda, mentioned earlier, catalyzed her own breakthrough by daring to send a heartfelt message after a workshop. My own habit of waiting for "the right mood"

CHAPTER 8: MINDSET MATTERS MOST

almost stopped me from attending a weekly group until I pushed through, shared openly, and someone offered me an opportunity. Through these repeated "micro-courage" actions, I built new skills and walked through open doors I couldn't have planned for.

Mike's transformation is another example. A coaching client of mine, he was initially hesitant to have honest, even difficult conversations with one of his clients. However, he decided to use consistent reflection and courageous conversations to solve old problems. This led to him building a reputation of honesty and integrity, and he became a resource for other clients. My own "aha moments" also happened when I stopped waiting to feel ready or perfect and just stepped in, reached out, followed up, or spoke up, in spite of unease.

Reader Reflection: Reflect on one habit that's keeping you from growing. Maybe it's skipping crucial follow-ups, holding back feedback, or ducking out of networking events too early. Challenge yourself to change that pattern just once this week. Write about your experience and results in your journal during your weekly review and reflection.

Movement, Self-Care & Your Empowerment Plan

Mindset isn't just a matter of thought; it's embodied in motion and self-care. My most creative ideas rarely surface while at my desk. They come when I'm on lunchtime walks, driving in silence, working out at the gym, or engaging in informal brainstorms with others. Physical movement has become one of my secret weapons—not only for boosting energy, but for unlocking perspective and using that to deepen relationships.

In the early stages of my real estate career, I revived a daily ritual: sending authentic check-in messages to colleagues or clients while on my walks. A quick "thinking of you" text had the potential to lead to a collaboration, a workshop, or referrals. These moments weren't scheduled, but they made all the difference because I consistently acted on my desire to reach out.

Self-care strategies like moving, being still, journaling, scheduling downtime, and practicing structured routines safeguard your energy and resilience. For example, after the county let me go from a counseling job—a deep blow—I gave myself permission to feel, reset, and recover. Anytime I've experienced failure or rejection, I've needed what I call "cave time," time to let myself feel fully, reflect deeply and gain clarity. This time was no different. Then, I returned to entrepreneurship with clearer focus and a renewed sense of purpose.

Using the SIDE and RADICAL Focus frameworks, I am able to blend strategic rest, movement, and vision planning into my routine. Before big events, I visualize

CHAPTER 8: MINDSET MATTERS MOST

connecting with confidence and authenticity—an exercise that's helped both me and clients connect. Small, consistent rituals build the momentum and confidence you need to step into new settings and roles.

Empowerment isn't a one-and-done experience; it's something you experience through a series of daily commitments. Whether it's a walk, a reflection break, or a celebration of your wins, these are the building blocks for impact, for yourself and your network.

Reader Reflection: Craft your own "empowerment hour" this week—combine movement, reflection, and outreach. Maybe it's an early morning walk, 10 minutes journaling accomplishments, or sending a gratitude message. Try it for a week and write about your experience and results.

By rooting your mindset in intentional stillness, focused action, courageous pattern-breaking, and movement, you unlock a wellspring of resilience and connection. All of my stories, including my failures, comebacks, client wins, and new connections, reinforce this truth: Positive, consistent internal shifts create external results. You're building not just skills, but a network and reputation of authenticity and trust.

The next step is to outline and create your mindset makeover blueprint. Start a self-care ritual, plan a weekly outreach that adds value, and find an accountability

133

partner who champions your growth. These are habits that will lead to empowerment. And when you make these habits the foundation of your journey, you're not only supporting your own transformation, you're elevating everyone around you.

Your choices build your journey toward a resilient and empowered mindset each moment, every day. Use the tools in this book to guide your actions, and remember: The rewards of growth extend far beyond business or networking. They ripple out, strengthening your community and creating success for you and those you're privileged to impact.

"Celebrate small achievements regularly to reinforce progress and remind yourself that every step forward matters."

As you step into the next chapter, get ready to put these principles into practice with concrete, step-by-step strategies for building authentic connections. You already have everything you need to create extraordinary relationships, starting with the mindset you choose, right now.

Chapter 9 will show you how to leverage this solid foundation to cultivate connections that elevate both your business and your life. Get ready to discover practical methods and strategies for making connections that help you, and those around you, succeed at every level.

Chapter 9: Networking for Introverts

When I started my networking journey, I hated it because it felt daunting and intimidating. The sea of handshakes, small talk, and crowded events didn't align with who I am at my core. Early on, these situations often left me drained and questioning if I was cut out to build connections in a way that felt real. My experience after the dot-com crash is a perfect example. I describe it as my origin story: Having lost my IT career overnight, I was forced into entrepreneurship and felt deeply out of place in networking crowds, engaging in surface-level interactions. But here's the truth I've come to understand: Networking as an introvert doesn't need to look the same as it does for extroverts. The real power comes not from changing who we are but from harnessing our natural strengths to forge authentic, meaningful connections. And that takes a strategic approach.

Networking isn't about being the loudest voice; it's about leaving an impact. That insight came to me many years later, after forming my first BNI chapter (a story you'll recall from Chapter 7). I learned that recognition and thoughtfulness, like publicly celebrating another's achievements or sending personalized follow-up notes, sparks connections that can lead to opportunities. After one networking event, I set myself apart not by working the room but by reaching out to a new acquaintance with an honest comment about their recent success. That act led to a connection, referrals, and eventually a partnership, proving that when you support others in subtle, genuine ways, your actions speak louder than self-promotion.

"Introversion is a strength—not a weakness—when it comes to building professional relationships. Lead with authenticity and quiet confidence."

Organization is a superpower for introverts. Early in my career, I kept a notebook (yup, real old school…) with birthdays, hobbies, and key moments from my networking conversations. That simple tool paid off. For example, after jotting down someone's career milestone, I sent a congratulatory note a week later—and that gesture became the foundation of a mentorship. Over time, these touches built a network that valued respect rather than obligation.

In this chapter, I want to help you shift from feeling overwhelmed to empowered in your networking journey. To do this, you'll need solid strategies for building your network and an understanding that the ability to stay true to yourself, even as you stretch and grow, is the greatest asset you will ever have. Now, let's take that next step and build your introvert-friendly networking strategy.

CHAPTER 9: NETWORKING FOR INTROVERTS

Implementing Strategies: Applying the Networking Framework

A sustainable networking strategy for introverts starts with thoughtful preparation and intentional action. Drawing from my own journey during my early years in real estate after the abrupt end of my IT career, I found that low-pressure environments sparked more meaningful connections. I also found that attending niche events, small gatherings, and even virtual or in-person coffee chats allowed me to ease into networking without feeling overwhelmed. On top of that, forming my own networking group by launching my first BNI chapter gave me the chance to strategically design my environment, choosing the size, scope, and format, which enabled me to grow in confidence and form connections as I grew at my own speed.

Intentional questions are important for mindful preparation. I enjoy using frameworks like FORD questions (family, occupation, recreation, and dreams) not just as ice-breakers, but as pathways to deeper connections. When I started using FORD questions, "small talk" became suuuuuper easy. Instead of worrying about what to say or ask, I let others share their stories, which took the pressure off of me while deepening the connection. At a real estate meet-up for instance, I was able to move past awkward intros by focusing on getting to know a colleague's journey. This led to an invitation to collaborate on a community service project later.

Taking action is the other key part of this strategy. Celebrating others and following up can be more effective than trying to "work the room." I once sent a message to a client I'd met briefly after hearing about their recent accomplishment. It opened the door to mentorship and reciprocal referrals. Who knew!

Evaluation and Adjustment: Reviewing and Improving Tactics

Effective networking is iterative; each connection is an opportunity to learn, adapt, and grow. After events I take time to reflect about what felt real to me, and what left me feeling out of alignment. This process, rooted in the mindset shifts from Chapter 8, has repeatedly pushed me forward. Keeping a journal of interactions, including wins, losses, and lessons I've learned, has also helped me tune into strategies that work with my energy and personality.

Asking myself questions like, "Did I prioritize *quality* connections?" and "Did I let my curiosity shine?" guides my growth. Years ago, during my corporate stint in the mid 90s at a pharmaceutical company called McKesson, I made informational interviews part of my self-evaluation and exploration. Tracking which connections led to mentorships, projects, or internal job opportunities taught me to focus less on quantity and more on the quality of the connection I was building.

If something didn't go well, like an event that left me feeling exhausted afterwards because I mimicked inauthentic behavior, I revised my approach. Each lesson,

CHAPTER 9: NETWORKING FOR INTROVERTS

whether from a misstep or a win, shaped my evolution and kept me connected and confident.

"Networking is best approached with clarity about your boundaries and energy levels. It's okay to focus on one meaningful connection rather than just seeking quantity."

Creating Community: Finding and Contributing to Supportive Circles

Consider the powerful difference between joining a massive event and intentionally cultivating your own supportive group, as I did with my BNI chapters. Founding these chapters showed me how much more we can achieve by focusing on quality over quantity. These groups are "lifelines" and places where I nurture trust, offer value, and build community.

Joining isn't enough; it's about making a contribution. I've seen firsthand that authentic offers of help, introductions, or tailored input can lead to more solid connections than I had when I spread myself thin. In weekly BNI meetings, I focused on connecting with just two or three people each time, always guided by the principle of adding value, whether it was an introduction, a resource, or simply a celebration of someone's win.

Over the years, many of these small circle connections have turned into trusted referral sources, supportive colleagues, and lifelong friends. The secret: Show up consistently, give what value you can, and treat each person as a partner, not just another name in your contact book.

Understanding the Power of Introversion in Networking

Introverts possess underestimated strengths that, when harnessed, redefine what successful networking looks like. I used to think that introversion was a deficit, not an asset. I learned over time that we're natural listeners and deep thinkers, and we excel at one-on-one or small group engagement. That insight hit me like a ton of bricks. My experiences showed me that these traits were assets. I learned to lean into active listening and intentional follow-up, building trust over time with new connections, peers, and clients. Taking baby steps, learning little by little, and growing at my pace was key to gaining these insights.

As I've shared, when I started over in real estate, I transformed my perceived "shyness" into an advantage by becoming the one who remembered details and followed up. Eye contact, open-ended questions, and honest curiosity helped me go deeper in conversations, even when nerves kicked in, which showed others I valued them.

Celebrating small wins, like sending notes or a handwritten card, has become one of my secret weapons as an introvert. Over time, people reciprocated this attention to detail with meaningful connections and invitations to events and opportunities. This is clear proof that you can build a powerful network without ever shouting to be heard.

 *Reader Reflection*: Think of a recent networking experience, noting your strengths and challenges as an introvert. What worked and what didn't? What did you learn about yourself?

Building Confidence and Authentic Connections

Most networkers have learned that confidence comes from practice, not perfection. We become more confident by finding ways to be authentic, rather than putting on a mask. To practice, I developed elevator pitches for many scenarios, as inspired by my years with BNI. In each meeting, my message evolved until it reflected not just what I did, but who I am and the value I offer. Practicing these made interactions less stressful and gave me the courage to connect in *my* voice, not the "perfect" script I thought people wanted to hear.

Preparation helps, also. Before events, I'd identify a few people I wanted to meet and then research them, which gave me tailored conversation starters and eased the anxiety of small talk. At larger gatherings, I set a modest "success" goal—say, one or two real connections—so I could celebrate progress, not berate myself if I didn't "work the room."

"Identify one or two people you want to speak to at networking events and create deeper connections through thoughtfully prepared FORD questions (family, occupation, recreation, dreams)."

Knowing my limits was equally important. I sometimes left events early after a few deep interactions, using simple lines with people like, "I'd love to reconnect soon." One of my favorite tricks is a "bathroom break." This is a discreet strategy that allows me time to chill and regroup without feeling awkward or overwhelmed.

As Chapter 8 highlighted, authentic connections grow from being yourself, showing up with curiosity and care, and following up consistently. None of these require you to act like an extrovert. Over time, small, genuine interactions can grow into a self-sustaining network—one that fuels your confidence and business growth.

Reader Reflection: Reach out to a friend or colleague for a one-on-one virtual coffee chat to practice networking. Journal about the experience and what you learned about yourself.

CHAPTER 9: NETWORKING FOR INTROVERTS

Mastering the Art of Listening and Conversation

The introvert superpower of active listening, which Chapter 2 explores more deeply, can become your sharpest tool in networking. While most folks focus on speaking, I learned (especially in my early realtor days) that making someone feel heard is a gift not many people give. Remembering details, echoing back what others share, or gently probing for more information ("What inspired you to start your business?") consistently deepened my conversations.

FORD questions (family, occupation, recreation, dreams) remain my go-to. I recall using them at a community event where the conversation lasted far longer than expected and I formed a connection, simply because I asked a volunteer about their family's role in their efforts. This approach is about cultivating sincere curiosity and giving the other person the gift of attention.

These habits, along with intentional silence, eye contact, and regular follow-up, help establish trust and make your conversations memorable. As a result, they turn acquaintances or sporadic contacts into true allies and advocates.

 *Reader Reflection*: Engage in a deep conversation with someone you haven't connected with recently and practice FORD questions (family, occupation, recreation, dreams) and active listening. Journal about the experience and identify what you learned about yourself.

Leveraging Introverted Networking Strategies

Traditional networking may not fit everyone's mold, and that's okay. I usually make a plan for events around my needs and comfort level, aiming for deeper connections instead of just more connections. My preferred strategies were: bringing along a "wing-person" (like a trusted friend I met when I opened my second BNI chapter), attending small groups, or choosing workshops over massive mixers.

During the pandemic, for example, my mastermind accountability partner and I would meet weekly for focused support and brainstorming. No crowds or forced conversations required—just consistent, powerful growth. This structure made networking not just manageable but also energizing and fun. Networking can also be one on one or in small groups with around three or four people, making it feel "safer" to connect meaningfully.

Online communities and meetings can be just as powerful. Participating in focused virtual groups for

CHAPTER 9: NETWORKING FOR INTROVERTS

marketing or real estate helped me connect with peers across the country who shared my values and goals. However, with these online communities, follow up is especially important. It reinforces the connection because, often, online interactions can be shallow. The key was always the same: Be strategic, stay authentic, pursue depth over breadth, and *consistently follow up*. Remember, fortune is in the follow up.

 Reader Reflection: Identify a potential strategic partner or business friend and reach out to initiate a conversation about a networking collaboration.

Crafting Your Networking Message and Elevator Pitch

Walking into a room, heart pounding and inner critic screaming, used to be my reality. Over time, I discovered that creating and rehearsing an elevator pitch—not a sales pitch, but an authentic snapshot of who I am, why I do what I do, and what value I bring—helped ground me. My multiple years with BNI made it so that I practice this skill all the time; refining and customizing my message has become second nature.

I have built a "library" of variations so I have a pitch for every context, from casual meet-ups to formal gatherings, and even social media posts. Each one expresses who I helped, what unique insights I bring to the table, and a clear call to action. Rehearsing these meant that when my nerves hit, I had something to lean on, and they helped others immediately understand the value I bring.

A great pitch is about being clear, honest, and memorable. It's not about being slick. When you find the words that fit, they become both a shield from nervousness and a bridge helping you connect faster and more intentionally.

Reader Reflection: Draft a 60-second elevator pitch that highlights your strengths and value proposition. Rewrite it two more times for different scenarios. Practice it in front of a mirror. Then, journal about your experience and what you discovered about yourself.

Building a Networking Strategy

Bringing all these elements together forms a personalized networking strategy—one grounded in intentionality, authenticity, and adaptability. In the early stages of my real estate career, I set clear goals for meeting new professionals, kept track of my progress, and regularly evaluated what was working and what wasn't. This helped me course-correct and double down on strategies that brought results, whether that meant deepening current connections or seeking new ones.

CHAPTER 9: NETWORKING FOR INTROVERTS

 *"Make sure to schedule breaks during larger networking events or set boundaries for leaving when your energy requires it. When you do this, you prioritize quality over time spent."*

I learned to research potential connections before reaching out, to find common interests and always be ready with a few conversation starters. If something wasn't clicking, if I started feeling drained by a large event for example, I gave myself permission to adjust my plan and make space for techniques that energized me instead.

Above all, I learned consistency was key. I follow up after meetings, check in periodically, and celebrate others' accomplishments. These small, consistent actions maintain my network and lead me to opportunities I couldn't have anticipated from the beginning.

 Reader Reflection: Outline your networking goals and create a one-year strategy. Journal about how this feels and what you've learned about yourself along the way.

Networking as an introvert isn't about forcing yourself into an extrovert's mold. It's about shaping a path around *your* strengths, values, and intentions. By embracing the frameworks, real-life examples, and strategies from my journey, you'll move forward equipped to build authentic, lasting, and mutually beneficial connections on your terms.

You've learned how to master the art of cultivating meaningful connections in person and virtually; now, it's time to take that confidence into the digital realm. In the next chapter, we'll explore how to carry this confidence and intentionality across all platforms, building camera presence and sharing your story. Stay empowered, stay motivated, and always remember that your introversion is a strength, not a limitation.

Chapter 10: Camera Confidence and Content

When I first began creating videos, I was riddled with self-doubt, uncertainty, and plenty of insecurities. I knew video content was a powerful tool, but I had no roadmap, no clear sense of purpose, and no real confidence in front of a camera. The idea of putting myself out there for an audience felt overwhelming. The irony is that I had some background in performance, like stage experience from theater classes, a history of singing in choirs, and experience shooting a few commercials, but none of that prepared me for the intricate dance of speaking to a camera completely alone.

Unlike the buzzing energy of a crowded auditorium, the solitude I experienced in a recording studio was both comforting and unnerving. Being an introvert didn't help either. The weight of potential judgment loomed large, making those early steps feel impossible.

Here's where connection and supportive community made all the difference. Early on, I heard a story from a colleague named Neal that inspired me. Neal was another introvert who had struggled taking the leap into video content. He shared how he felt invisible in a sea of gregarious personalities, and how that insecurity nearly kept him from pressing the record button. What ultimately shifted things for him was a simple message he received from someone in his network: "Your story matters—and it might be exactly what someone else needs to hear." That one comment sparked his courage to post his first video. His vulnerable, honest approach built loyalty and attracted countless messages from viewers who felt empowered to share their own stories.

Embracing this same spirit, I pressed on. I immersed myself in learning by watching others succeed, taking courses, and absorbing knowledge from experts like YouTube coach Tim Schmoyer with Video Creators (now vidIQ). I drew from my Toastmasters experience, which taught me structure, how to be calm under pressure, and the tools to present confidently to any room. I also leveraged stories I'd collected from my network, and noticed a pattern. Every creator, regardless of their personality type, hit roadblocks of insecurity and fear. But those who persisted did so with the encouragement and feedback from others.

 "Your story matters—and it might be exactly what someone else needs to hear."

Even now, with years of practice under my belt, I want to emphasize this fundamental truth: Fear and nervousness never truly disappear. They're part of the process. Your amygdala's fight-or-flight response triggers a rush of adrenaline—that's normal and it's also a sign that you care. Overcoming these feelings doesn't mean eliminating them. It means finding the courage to act

CHAPTER 10: CAMERA CONFIDENCE AND CONTENT

in spite of them. Courage isn't about being fearless; it's about showing up and moving forward, even when fear accompanies you.

In fact, a story from my network sparked one of the most memorable moments in my journey. A peer, Sarah, recounted her struggle with camera shyness. She shared that in order to overcome this, she set a challenge to record one video every day for 30 days. It didn't matter if they were perfect, or even if she posted them—what mattered was the repetition, the willingness to record regularly. By the end of the month, because of her consistent practice and effort, not only had her confidence bloomed, but her authentic stories fostered genuine connections and conversations online. Witnessing this transformation reminded me that our willingness to practice, even imperfectly, is what fuels growth and opportunity.

This chapter is the culmination of my experiences to date with lessons learned, mistakes made, and victories won, as well as the stories of others who found their courage through connection. If you've struggled with camera anxiety or content insecurity, know that you're not alone. I've been there, and I've built a simple, effective framework—the MVP framework—to help others just like you break through barriers holding them back. MVP stands for "myths, voice, and plan." Throughout this chapter, I'll walk you through these essential pillars so that you, too, can create impactful content that aligns with your personality and passion. Whether you're shy or simply unsure about your message, there's a path forward. Together, we'll dispel harmful myths, discover your authentic voice, and craft a solid plan for success.

This is your invitation to step into your potential. Are you ready? Then, let's do this.

Dispelling Myths

The first barrier you will likely face isn't technical—it's mental. It sure was for me; imposter syndrome kicked in big time. Before you even hit record, you've probably told yourself stories about why you can't succeed in front of a camera. These thoughts are dangerous because they feel so real, but they're nothing more than myths we've come to believe over time. They come from fear and insecurity, and if you leave them unchecked, they can stop you from ever starting.

One of the biggest myths I've encountered is the belief that introverts can't thrive on video. Let me tell you—that's absolute horse-pucky. I know because I'm proof. I'm deeply introverted, and for years, I believed that my shy nature was a weakness, especially in spaces that extroverts dominated. But I've learned something important: Introversion can be an incredible tool for creating impactful content. While extroverts might draw energy from an audience, introverts have a unique ability to focus deeply, create authentic connections, and communicate meaningful, reflective messages. Introverts often bring thoughtfulness and intentionality to their work, which can really resonate with viewers.

Stories from my network continue to challenge these limiting beliefs. For example, after I hosted a virtual networking event, a participant shared with me

CHAPTER 10: CAMERA CONFIDENCE AND CONTENT

how nervous she'd been to introduce herself on camera. Yet, just hearing a few kind words from other attendees about her "genuine authenticity" instantly reframed her mindset. She realized that vulnerability is often the best bridge to connection, online and offline. Her story serves as a reminder that self-perceived weaknesses can, in fact, be our greatest strengths in a world craving authenticity.

And let me clear up another misconception: Insecurity isn't exclusive to introverts. Extroverts get anxious, too. They might appear more confident, but even the most outgoing person can feel the pressure of being in front of a camera. If someone tells you they never feel nervous, they're probably lying. I still get insecure from time to time and I have hundreds of videos under my belt! The key to overcoming this barrier is understanding that everyone—yes, everyone—is fighting their own internal battles. With time and practice, your insecurities will get quieter, but they may never leave completely. Just know you're not an anomaly. Your feelings of fear or self-doubt don't mean you aren't capable. They just mean you're human.

"Fear and nervousness never truly disappear. Courage isn't about being fearless; it's about showing up and moving forward, even when fear accompanies you."

Another common myth I see holding people back is the idea that your content must be groundbreaking or revolutionary to matter. This belief paralyzes so many people before they even begin because they think their message isn't "big" enough. That was me for sure! I thought I had to have a groundbreaking idea or topic to talk about. But here's the truth: You don't need to reinvent the wheel. You just need to connect with your audience by being authentic. Speak about your passions, your experiences, your lessons, and the problems you've overcome. People really want to hear about the messy crap because that's what they relate to! Not the perfect stuff that's really baloney. Share things that matter to you in a way that's real. Authenticity is what resonates with people, not perfection or flashiness. So, be yourself unabashedly!

What many people don't realize is that viral success isn't a magic formula. People who are overnight successes are usually anomalies anyway, reaching success unintentionally. It's not about creating something that's never been done before. Viral success is often the byproduct of consistently showing up, being real, and creating connections through that realness with your audience. Over time, that consistency builds trust and loyalty, and that's far more valuable than any quick burst of attention.

A memorable story that illustrates this is from Marcus, who would freeze at every "go live" button. Then, instead of waiting for the perfect moment or script, Marcus challenged himself to engage with his community on a weekly basis, sharing one authentic takeaway from his networking experiences. He wasn't polished at first but connecting with his audience authentically and

CHAPTER 10: CAMERA CONFIDENCE AND CONTENT

consistently led to collaborations and later, opportunities to speak at other events.

So, don't let these myths stop you. Introvert or extrovert, groundbreaking content or simple stories—what matters is that you show up, share your voice, and stay true to yourself. That's how you break through the mental barriers and start creating content that truly makes an impact.

Finding Your Voice

Once you've dismantled limiting myths, you can uncover your voice. Your voice is the heartbeat of your content. It's your perspective, your experiences, your passions, all distilled into a message that only you can deliver. It's what makes your message resonate and stand out in a sea of content. Your voice is the bridge between you and your audience, creating a connection that inspires trust, relatability, and engagement. However, finding your voice takes time, effort, practice, and patience. It's not as easy as flipping a switch; you develop this skill through practice. Don't expect perfection from Day One. It's okay to stumble; it's okay to feel awkward; it's okay to hate the sound of your own voice on playback (we all do at first). What matters is that you keep going and commit to the process.

Repetition is the best teacher. The more you record and experiment, the more natural and confident you will feel over time. Start small by practicing in front of a mirror, recording bite-sized clips on your phone, or even speaking your thoughts out loud as you go about your day.

These small, intentional steps can act as building blocks, helping you become more comfortable with expressing yourself. When I started out, it took me forever to record five minutes of content. I would record and re-record and re-record, seeking that perfect take. It was exhausting and frustrating, but I slowly got to the place where I could let the camera roll. I learned to practice being myself rather than getting it perfect.

Another key practice: watching your footage. Yes, it can be excruciating and uncomfortable at first, but self-review is where the magic happens. It's the moment you start to truly identify your strengths and pinpoint areas for improvement. Watching yourself allows you to see what works, what doesn't, and where we need to grow. Look for patterns. Are there moments when your energy spikes or dips? Are you communicating clearly? Are your gestures and expressions complementing your words? These observations will help you refine your approach and adjust.

Throughout my networking experiences, I've learned how vital it is to let my personality and style shine, even if it feels unconventional or uncomfortable, and this applies to video especially. Kristin, a close professional connection, shared that she used to carefully script every line before recording, thinking that "getting it right" mattered most. But it wasn't until she let go of the script and spoke candidly about a challenge she faced in her business that her audience began to engage. The positive response was heartwarming, and her story reached further than any of her polished, scripted content ever had. This reinforces what I want you to remember:

CHAPTER 10: CAMERA CONFIDENCE AND CONTENT

Your audience is drawn to your authenticity, not your perfection.

Don't forget to seek feedback from others—coaches, mentors, colleagues, and even trusted friends and family. Outside perspectives provide insights you may have overlooked, helping you uncover blind spots in order to refine your delivery. Receiving constructive criticism isn't always easy; it can feel uncomfortable or even discouraging. But it's one of the most powerful tools for growth. Embracing feedback with an open mind allows you to improve in ways you might not on your own. Remember, no one starts out as a master. Everyone who has found their voice has taken this same journey filled with trials, errors, and discoveries.

Most importantly, be patient and kind to yourself. Developing your voice is an evolving process, and every step you take brings you closer to owning your unique style. Celebrate your progress, no matter how small, and don't compare your Chapter One to someone else's Chapter 10. Remember, no one else can tell your story the way you can—that's what makes your voice unique. It's not just about speaking; it's about sharing something that is authentically you with the world. So embrace the journey, trust the process, and let your voice shine.

"Repetition is your best teacher, and consistency is key. Every video you create, every blog post you write, and every piece of content you share is a step toward mastery."

Planning Your Content Creation

Now that belief and authenticity are in place, it's time to add structure. Planning is the backbone of consistency, and consistency is what builds an engaged and loyal audience over time. Without a solid plan, it's easy to lose momentum and let your efforts fizzle out.

Start by identifying topics that align with *your* interests, expertise, and the value you want to bring to your audience. Think about the questions your clients or community commonly ask, the ones that keep popping up. What challenges have you personally overcome that others can relate to? These experiences are a goldmine for content ideas. Take the time to create a master list of these topics, and don't just stop there—organize and prioritize them based on relevance, audience needs, and your enthusiasm for sharing them. The more passionate you are about a topic, the more it will shine through in your content.

Scheduling is equally important. If you don't block time in your calendar to plan, write, and record content, it won't happen. I want to repeat that: *If you don't block time in your calendar to plan, write, and record content, it won't happen.* Treat it like any other important meeting or task. Dedicate specific time slots to brainstorm ideas, create content, and refine your content. This level of intentionality will ensure efforts remain consistent and productive even when life gets busy.

In my own journey, and the journeys of those shared by my network, I have seen repeatedly that

CHAPTER 10: CAMERA CONFIDENCE AND CONTENT

intentional planning is the key difference between abandoned ideas and completed projects. For example, one networking colleague built a content calendar around the topics that excited her most, starting with just one video a week. That commitment, rooted in her desire to serve her audience, led to a steady stream of followers and growing confidence on camera. Her content didn't just "happen"—it was the direct result of small, intentional steps backed by intentional planning.

While I'm a fan of leveraging tools like AI to streamline the content creation process, I want to caution you against losing your authentic voice in the shuffle. AI can be an incredible assistant for things like brainstorming ideas, drafting outlines, or refining language, but your audience is tuning in for *you—your* perspective, *your* experiences, *your* unique personality. A robotic-sounding script will never resonate, so aim to strike a balance between using technology to assist and staying true to yourself. Let AI support you, but you must let *your* authentic voice lead the way.

It's also important to remember that consistency matters more than volume. You don't need to post every single day to make an impact, but you do need to honor a rhythm your audience can rely on. Posting consistently helps establish trust and visibility over time. It also signals to your audience that you're reliable, which is crucial for maintaining engagement. And don't just post; engage with your audience. Respond to comments, ask questions, and encourage real conversations. Social media algorithms thrive on meaningful interactions, and so does your audience. Adding a simple call-to-action

(CTA) at the end of your posts, like asking a question, inviting feedback, or encouraging shares, can work wonders for fostering engagement. Whether it's "What's your take on this?" or "Share your own experience below," small efforts go a long way.

 "Start small, even if it's just one video, one post, or one small step toward your goal. Stay consistent, and you'll begin to see your efforts build momentum over time."

Final Thoughts

The main takeaways here are simple but powerful. First, nerves are normal. Expect them and move forward anyway. Feeling nervous or unsure is part of the process, and everyone feels self-conscious and insecure at first. Those initial jitters don't define you. The most important thing is to not let that fear hold you back.

Second, stop fixating on how you look or sound. It's easy to overanalyze yourself, but trust me, everyone feels the same way when they're starting out. The truth is, most people are focused on the value of what you're saying, not minor details like your tone or appearance, or whether you're perfect or not. Once you start creating content regularly, you'll gain confidence naturally and those worries will start to fade. If that can happen for me, then it can happen for you!

CHAPTER 10: CAMERA CONFIDENCE AND CONTENT

Finally, repetition is your best teacher, and consistency is the key. Every video you create, every blog post you write, and every piece of content you share is a step toward mastery. Each time you put yourself out there, you're learning, improving, and becoming more comfortable in the process. Growth happens steadily when you keep showing up.

Remember, you don't have to go at this alone. Some of the most committed, insightful content creators I know attribute their progress to the support and accountability that came from their coaches, mentors, and networks. As one of them shared with me, a peer group challenge to post weekly videos led to breakthroughs that wouldn't have occurred in isolation. Lean into your community, let others cheer you on, and return the favor by supporting others in their creative process. Valuable networking is never just about the numbers—it's about connection, community, encouragement, and growth.

You already have the tools, the framework, and the ability to succeed. It's all there waiting for you. The only thing left is to take action. Start small, even if it's just one video, one post, or one small step toward your goal. Stay consistent, and you'll begin to see your efforts build momentum over time. You've got this, and your journey is just getting started!

So to repeat:

- We're all nervous, it's freaking normal.   GET OFF IT!
- None of us like what we look like or sound like on camera.   GET OVER IT!
- Repetition (practice) builds confidence.   GET INTO IT!

This chapter was a reflection on my journey and a roadmap for your content creation success. We dove into the challenges and triumphs that come with creating content, covering insights and actionable advice to help along the way. We tackled myths that often hold creators back, such as the belief that you need to have everything perfect before you start, and we explored how to uncover and embrace what makes your voice unique—because your individuality is your greatest asset.

Together, we laid out a reliable plan to help you move forward with purpose and direction, focusing on clarity and consistency. By now, you've gained tools to approach video creation with more confidence, clarity, and creativity, allowing you to step into the process with a renewed sense of enthusiasm.

It's important to remember that no one starts as an expert. It's through consistent practice, trial and error, and a commitment to improvement that you'll continue to grow and refine your craft. The key is to push past the initial fear, the insecurity that tells you to stop before you've even started, and step into a space where your authentic self can shine. This is the space where the

CHAPTER 10: CAMERA CONFIDENCE AND CONTENT

magic happens, where your unique perspective resonates with an audience that's been waiting for someone just like you.

Keep in mind, this journey is about connecting, inspiring, and building something that reflects who you are. It's not just about content creation. The path won't always be easy, but the rewards of expressing your unique voice and seeing it impact others will make it all worthwhile. So take a deep breath, lean into the process, and embrace the journey ahead. Let's keep building!!

Conclusion: Becoming Your Best Self

Reflecting on my 25-year entrepreneurial journey, I recognize that every milestone and every challenge has shaped the professional I am today. Circumstances first thrust me into entrepreneurship as an introvert before I felt ready, and the road ahead felt overwhelming and isolating. But time and experience showed me that success comes from showing up, staying true to my values, and taking action even when the path is unclear. I found my strengths not by mimicking others, but by listening deeply, reflecting before acting, and building relationships that matter.

Some of my greatest breakthroughs came through small, meaningful interactions, turning connections that seemed fleeting into lifelong friendships and invaluable partnerships. These moments taught me the most powerful truth of all: Success is not about perfection. It's about consistent progress, a willingness to learn, and having the courage to act while honoring your own authentic self.

The Power of Progress

Small steps often disguise progress. My own journey—from navigating the chaos of the dot.com crash era and wrestling through licensing exams to learning the art of networking as an introvert and ultimately becoming the Bowtie Coach—demonstrates that every win and every setback holds a lesson. Remember Tom's story, about a relationship that started with a handwritten follow-up note after a quick introduction. That act led to a mentorship that changed my business and my outlook on life.

Every challenge, whether it's overcoming fears of rejection, missing out on an opportunity, or pushing through failure, becomes fuel for personal growth and resilience. Much like Linda, the health coach who transformed a chance conversation into a lasting partnership through simple, well-timed follow-ups, you too can create shifts in your journey by valuing progress over perfection.

I encourage you to try this exercise: Take a moment to write a letter to your future self, five years ahead. Describe not only the achievements you hope to realize, but the person you aspire to become, the relationships you want to deepen, and the new challenges you will embrace. Use this letter as a touchstone and a pledge to yourself that progress, more than outcomes, will define your story.

Staying Grounded Amid Success

Sustained success requires more than hustle; it demands that you stay grounded in habits and relationships that nourish your spirit. In the rush to "make it," it's easy to overlook the core practices that keep you energized and emotionally resilient. I've watched clients and colleagues burn out by chasing every new goal or shiny object without tending to their own well-being, and truthfully, I've been there myself. The lesson? Lasting achievement comes from prioritizing self-care just as much as your next breakthrough.

Whether it's intentionally scheduling coffee or lunch dates to nurture key relationships (just as I did with former acquaintances who became essential parts of my support network), or setting clear boundaries around work and downtime, these habits will help you thrive over the long term. One of the most profound stories I've witnessed is from a former client who made celebrating small wins, theirs and others, a ritual in both life and business. Their appreciation deepened their relationships and established them as a trusted connector, creating ripple effects far beyond anything they could have managed alone.

Ask yourself: What habits, rituals, and relationships will help you create balance as you continue to grow? Write these down and commit to treating them as non-negotiables in your pursuit of success.

Inviting the Journey

As you read this, I also invite you to pause and ask: What's been holding you back from taking that first, bold step? Is it fear, uncertainty, or the belief that your voice isn't enough? I've had those same doubts. But experience, and stories from many introverted, remarkable entrepreneurs

I've met, prove that quiet strength, listening, and authenticity are unbeatable in the long run.

You are not lacking because you're different. The world needs more introverted leaders, more connectors who build trust through follow-through and care. Remember Linda's and Tom's stories, which both centered on connections that flourished through notes, thoughtful follow-ups, celebrating others' wins, and small, purposeful actions. That's real influence. That's how you build impact and legacy.

Let me encourage you, like I do with my clients on the edge of their next breakthrough:

You are not broken because you're an introvert. You possess a strength and perspective that no one else can offer. Your unique approach allows you to build trust, create authentic connections, and create value in ways others cannot. Commit to intentional action today, however small—whether it's sending a note, reaching out for a coffee chat, or sharing your message in your own style. Progress is permissionless. Growth is a journey, not a final destination, and every genuine step puts you further along the path.

You are enough, just as you are. The world needs your vision and your way of leading. So start today, and trust that everything you need is already within you.

CONCLUSION: BECOMING YOUR BEST SELF

Key Points and Takeaways

- **Mindset Precedes Achievement:** Sustainable growth starts with self-awareness and the belief that you can change, learn, and thrive.

- **Progress Over Perfection:** Every step, no matter how small, moves you forward. Your journey is unique; honor the pace and the lessons.

- **Authentic Connections Are Your Secret Weapon:** Trust, follow-ups, and thoughtful gestures make up the currency that builds influence.

- **Systems Empower You; They Don't Limit You:** Leverage organized follow-ups, consistent self-care, and focused routines to sustain momentum without losing yourself in the process.

- **Action Brings Clarity:** You don't need to have everything figured out. Take imperfect action. With each step, the path becomes clearer.

- **Celebrate Yourself and Your Community:** Honor your wins, big and small. Lift others as you rise.

Next Steps

If you're ready to turn your strengths into unstoppable entrepreneurial power, I've created additional resources to help jumpstart your transformation:

- Opt in to the **newsletter** at www.bowtiecoach.com/optin.
- Download the free guide "**Networking for Introverts**" at www.bowtiecoach.com/guide.
- And for those who want a community to take their skills even further, join **LimitLESS Ignite**, a community designed for introverted entrepreneurs ready to connect with likeminded professionals and build their business with purpose. Visit www.bowtiecoach.com/ignite to learn more.

Under Construction:

- Take the **Mindset Makeover Course**, a deep-dive into rewiring your thinking for lasting success at www.bowtiecoach.com/mindset-makeover.
- Become a networking ninja with the **Networking for Introverts Course**, www.bowtiecoach.com/N4I
- Master your on-camera presence with the course **Camera Confidence & Content**, perfect for introverts ready to dominate video content at www.bowtiecoach.com/ccc

This is your invitation. Take it. Step into your power and transform your dreams into reality now. By tapping into your quiet strength, building authentic relationships, and nurturing a resilient mindset, you are already on the path to becoming your best self—building a business and life that leaves a lasting legacy. Enjoy the journey!

About the Author

Stephen Burchard (that's pronounced "Stefen"—don't worry, everyone gets it wrong the first time) has spent a lifetime evolving, reinventing, and occasionally tripping over his own shoelaces on the way to personal and professional growth. A lifelong lover of writing, research, and history, he is a quietly curious, introvert entrepreneur who finds paradise in the written word and the rabbit holes of learning.

His path has never been straight. More like a spiritual zigzag—part reinvention, part divine nudge, and part "Okay, Higher Power, I get it." He went from shy IT guy to reluctant entrepreneur, from surviving the dot-com collapse to thriving in real estate, from wallflower networker to bowtie-wearing coach for quiet leaders. Each twist shaped him. Each setback refined him. And each chapter taught him the same lesson: joy isn't a destination;it's in the journey.

Writing this book was another unexpected bend in the road. For years, self-doubt told him he wasn't "writer enough," "expert enough," or "worthy-of-being-read enough." Then he realized something simple and slightly hilarious: He *loves* writing. He loves the quiet, the flow, the creativity, the stillness. So he stopped fighting it. And "Networking for Introverts" became the proof.

Today, Stephen lives in Cathedral City in the sun-soaked Palm Springs region of California with his husband and their beloved fur baby—a trio that has fully embraced desert sunsets, gratitude practices, and the kind of everyday stillness that fuels both clarity and courage. Spiritual study, reflection, and quiet mornings aren't just routines; they're the bedrock of his businesses, his coaching, and the way he moves through the world.

This book is part memoir, part roadmap, and part breakthrough. It's a blend of lived experience, spiritual growth, decades of entrepreneurial reinvention, and the kind of lightly self-deprecating humor only someone who's failed a licensing exam *twice* and still came out wiser can offer.

And trust him ... this book won't be his last. The writing bug has officially taken hold. (He's already outlining Book #2—quietly, of course.)

Endorsements

Stefen Rey's readable, myth busting, step-by-step instructions for the self-promotionally challenged bring a rare humanity to the subject. In *Networking for Introverts - Connections Made Simple*, Stefen uses his own journey from introverted to confident to map out a path for anyone looking for inspiration.

—**Andrew Rohrer**, author of *A Fellowship of the Ashes*, and former family counselor at Hazelden Betty Ford Center

Stefen exemplifies what happens when curiosity, compassion, and courage meet real-world practice. Over the past year, I've witnessed his willingness to stretch, grow, and embrace challenge with purpose and humility. *Networking for Introverts - Connections Made Simple* reflects the same spirit he brings to his leadership—intentional, reflective, and deeply human. Leaders looking for a fresh perspective on connection will find Stefen's voice both relatable and encouraging.

—**Colleen Hauk**, *Founder and CEO, The Corporate Refinery*

"*Networking for Introverts - Connections Made Simple* will help anyone thrive in a world the seems to celebrate (and reward) extroverts. This book is raw, vulnerable, and powerful. It reveals a clear path to help introverts and extroverts to thrive in sales, entrepreneurship, business, and leadership. This book is for anyone willing to take action to overcome insecurities, eliminate imposter syndrome, and take charge of their future."

—**ERIK SEVERSEN**, Author of *Ordinary to Extraordinary*, TEDx Speaker

Stephen Burchard does not advise you to become an extrovert. Rather, he provides a practical, encouraging roadmap for building real relationships, quietly, confidently, and on your own terms. If networking has ever felt performative or draining, this book offers a better way to create authentic connections supported by simple frameworks you can actually use.

—**Gary Chefetz**, Author of *Creative Financing Handbook for Real Estate Professionals*

www.ingramcontent.com/pod-product-compliance
Lightning Source LLC
Chambersburg PA
CBHW070627030426
42337CB00020B/3945